no one is a stranger

no one

is a

stranger

FINDING LOVE, CONNECTION,
AND A BRILLIANT LIFE

monty moran

LIONCREST
PUBLISHING

NO ONE IS A STRANGER

Finding Love, Connection, and a Brilliant Life

FIRST EDITION

ISBN 978-1-5445-4232-4 Hardcover
      978-1-5445-4231-7 Paperback
      978-1-5445-4230-0 Ebook
      978-1-5445-4233-1 Audiobook

Contents

Preface

In 2015, my father, David Taylor Moran, died. It all happened very fast. Two weeks before he died, he was swimming in the warm waters off Maui, Hawaii and playing guitar with friends in the evenings. It was his idea of heaven. Then, suddenly, he developed a lung infection. When I called from Colorado to say hi, I quickly knew something was wrong. My dad very seldom complained about his health, but when I asked him, "How are you doing?" he said (using my childhood nickname that never faded), "Well Moose, not great!" Such a comment might seem benign to most people, but I was alarmed to hear this from my dad.

"Should I come get you?" I asked, knowing full well he'd quickly say no and reassure me he'd be just fine.

"Wow, Moose, would you be willing to do that?" he answered.

I caught the next flight to Hawaii. My father had developed a terrible lung infection and was not able to get enough oxygen. The strong, sturdy man I'd so long looked up to could hardly move without becoming dangerously winded. I had to lift him onto the airplane with a narrow wheelchair and roll him down the aisle.

The flight back was pleasant. Actually, it was fun. I'd bought a bunch of Chinese food, and we feasted and talked the whole way. We were sure he'd be fine when he got back to his doctor in Colorado. Maybe he needed some steroids or something. He was going to be just fine. We were optimistic and excited.

But he wasn't fine. Once back in Colorado, the pulmonologist quickly pronounced he had "end stage pulmonary fibrosis."

"'End stage?'" I challenged the doctor. "How could it be 'end stage' if he was just fine a few days ago?"

I never got an answer to help me fully understand why I was losing my father at the age of seventy-five, when he seemed to be doing so well.

Over the next two weeks I watched the life fade out of him. I watched his breathing become more labored. I watched him die. But I also had two weeks to share nearly every minute with him. I even had the opportunity to ask him, point blank, "Dad, is there anything left that we need to say to each other?"

"No, Moose. I sure love you."

"I love you too, Dad, so much. You've been an incredible father. Thank you so much!"

We were able to have that time. We had those words. We had laughs, we had tears, and we had closure. I was able to say goodbye. Although I never actually said "goodbye."

Even as this heart-wrenching story played out, I noticed something extraordinary as my father stopped breathing and they took his lovely body away. I noticed that he was still with me. Not physically. Not in a ghostly sort of way. But in my heart. In the sunrise the next morning. In the knowledge that I carried with me. I even started to see more redtail hawks flying over me, almost daily. My dad had been an avid and passionate falconer. And as amazing as it sounds, all of his close friends shared this experience as well. Lots of encounters with hawks. All of us talked about how he was still with us.

Is this some sort of magic? Some sort of wishful thinking? Am I just using fantasy to avoid feeling profound pain and personal grief? I hope that by the time you've read this book you won't think so. You will understand my experience to be the truth.

Shortly after my dad died, I had dinner with my friend Stephanie, who also recently had lost her father. Of course, she was still mourning his loss, and as we spoke more I saw that she was really hurting about it. I shared my feelings about how, while we'd lost our fathers in the physical realm, their spirits lived on. I asked her, didn't she feel warmed by her father's spirit living on in her heart?

"Not at all," Stephanie said.

I was taken aback. "Really?"

She told me how she'd been so close to him, and that his death had left her permanently shattered and lonely. It left a hole in her heart that would not heal. She didn't feel that she'd ever be the same. To comfort her, I shared my deep belief that death is not the end of anything. To the contrary, death releases one's spirit so that it is no longer limited by the body and can be one with all life and with the universe. I told her how, in this respect, we might even find our fathers' deaths to allow us a closer relationship with them. We might feel an even deeper fulfillment in our heart. Stephanie seemed comforted by my words…at least somewhat.

When we parted, I encouraged her to see death not as an end of a person's journey, even if it was painful for those of us who remain to cope with the lack of a physical person to continue to spend time with.

This experience woke me up to how differently two people could choose to understand and cope with the death of their father. I realized that my particular understanding of reality provided me a lot more comfort and peace in the way I lived my life. I wanted her to have the same peace. The same comfort. I didn't want her to hurt forever, based on what I believe was a misunderstanding. I wanted her to see reality as I did, both because I believe my outlook is more accurate, and because I believe others who see things my way can live a much more fulfilling and harmonious and exciting existence.

The basis of my approach to life is the way I understand and define love, and the human relationships that so beautifully allow us to cultivate a closer relationship with love. To me, the purpose of our lives as human beings is to learn to become closer to the force that we call love, which means to become closer to the truth. Or to God. To me, as I will explain in this book, these three things (truth, love, and God) are one and the same.

The way we approach the subject of love will have a profound effect on how we live our lives. And the way we relate to others likewise will have a profound effect, since one of the most powerful ways we get in touch with the truth that is love that is God is through connections and relationships with the people around us. Great relationships help us to dwell in the comforting and beautiful realm of love. Deepening our understanding of love will help us to develop more of these connections. Relationships help us find love, and love helps us find relationships. It is a virtuous cycle, and I am convinced that focusing on these two things, love and relationships, will dramatically enrich all of our lives. I am convinced that this is the most important thing for each of us, as well as for our communities, businesses, organizations, and nations.

This is why I wrote this book.

Introduction

Since I was a young boy, people have often asked me why I'm always so happy and energetic. Only recently have I taken the time to consider what it is that causes people to have this impression. The answer is that I feel a deep connection to the people and the world around me.

The truth is I am not always happy. Like all of us, I often struggle with difficult feelings. Life is complex, and being happy all the time isn't a realistic goal. But no matter what I am feeling, I know that my focus on connecting with people and the world around me, and the deep relationships that result from this focus, will ground me, fulfill me, and make my life rich and rewarding.

Everyone struggles, and everyone wants to feel a sense of joy, meaning and fulfillment. We want this so badly that we'll try almost anything. But what I consistently see is that we tend to look in the wrong places to find it.

The key to unlocking a brilliant life is easily within reach for all of us. That key is the ability to connect deeply with the people and world around us. This connection, and a focus on cultivating the relationships that result from this connection, is the key to finding the power within us, and to finding that sense of joy and fulfillment which we all crave so badly.

In short, the quality of our life experience depends on the quality of this connection, and our relationships.

In my book, *Love is Free, Guac Is Extra*, I highlighted the difference between management and leadership, describing how management is about manipulating people, and is therefore ultimately ineffective. On the other hand, leadership requires developing genuine relationships which empower team members to achieve their own dreams while bringing success to your business. In other words, relationships are at the very core of business success. But **Love is Free** didn't tell the whole story.

The truth is that the only way to have an extraordinary life is to have extraordinary relationships. Great relationships are the key to succeeding in every aspect of life, whether it be our business, personal life, or spiritual life.

When we fail to establish this connection, it is painful. We feel a sense of being lost, lonely, even desperate. In this place, the happiness we long for seems only a distant dream. But the stakes are much higher than mere happiness. As a society, our lack of connection is already inflicting serious harm. There is significant evidence that we are presently the most narcissistic society in history. As a result, rates of depression, anxiety, drug overdose, and suicide are at epidemic levels. These problems arise because we are not developing the relationships which form the backbone of human wellness. We are not connecting like we could with others, resulting in a lack of community, disengaged workers, and dysfunctional families, businesses, and government. The way to change all of this starts with you and me.

When each of us sets our focus on building stronger connections and stronger relationships, each of us can begin to transform the quality of our lives, and, as a further result, we will begin to transform our society.

So this book is about you. It is about helping you to find brilliance in your life by harnessing the infinite power and love that will arise when you can more effectively feel the connection I am speaking about. It's about overcoming the obstacles that interfere with your connections with the people and world around you, to unleash a fullness and radiance that you would have never thought possible. Nothing is more important than this. Not only for you, but for the healthy development of our society, which is completely dependent upon the capability of each of us to carry it to a better place.

You need to be at your best, and this book is about helping you get there. What will unlock your brilliance is not limited to having a great connection with your parents, children, friends, partners, and spouses. Every encounter with every person is a chance for you to further this connection, feel your inner brilliance, and experience greatness. The best way to accomplish this is to think and act differently, and by doing so, to invite the power of love into your life.

I define love very differently than most do, and I will dive deeply into this subject in a moment. But for now, think of love as the greatest force in the world: that which gives you power, clarity, energy, brilliance, authenticity, and a foundation under your feet. The purpose of this book is to help you unlock this power. Through learning to foster a deeper connection with yourself and the world around you, you can literally become a powerhouse of love, warmth, support, goodness, radiance, and joy. There's nothing more important than this.

Because connecting to the power of love is so critical, I'm going to jump right in to offer a different way to look at this often used, but little understood concept. Then, I will address the greatest obstacle to connecting to others and to the power of love: that voice in your head that is critical, dissatisfied, and always chases the wrong goals: the ego. Finally, I will talk about a number of specific obstacles that all of us must confront on our journey to unlocking our own brilliance.

I've been so fortunate to find myself in positions where I was able to empower people to become better versions of themselves, not only as a CEO, but through deep connections with my friends, family, and community. I have always done this by focusing on deeper connections, and stronger relation-ships. I hope that by the time you finish this book, you'll have a different perspective on love and live more fully in its warm embrace. I hope you'll feel deeper connections with everyone and everything around you. I hope you'll find new relationships and resolve broken or strained relationships. I hope you'll find greater love for yourself, so you may find joy and fulfillment within. And, overall, I hope this book will help you feel seen, valued, understood, and loved so that you can blossom as a wellspring of vibrance and positivity for the benefit of yourself and the world around you.

CONNECTION

Today, the words *connection* or *connected* are used primarily to describe our link to the digital world. If I asked anyone on the street in most areas of the world, "Are you connected?", they would immediately think of Wi-Fi or cell phone connectivity.

Imagine how different the answer to this question would've been fifty years ago. We had no Wi-Fi, no cell phones, no social media. We had no way of learning current events beyond radio, TV, newspapers, and landline telephones. Back then, if someone had asked me "Are you connected" I am not sure what I would have said. "Connected to what?", perhaps.

In this book, I use the word "connected" to simultaneously discuss our connection to other people and our connection to something greater: a force that exists independent of us that can be harnessed to live a much more powerful and fulfilling life. Connections with people are at the foundation of great relationships. So when I talk about relationships, I am referring to an ongoing connection we have with certain people in our lives.

When I was a boy, interpersonal connections had a very different character than they do today. Besides the alarm clock, there were few if any interruptions by technology. No pings and beeps. No phones at the dinner table. When we were together, we were usually looking at each other, talking, and getting to know each other better.

We have evolved into a digital age, with technology that connects us to every corner of the earth, and with nearly every person. For the first time in history, the primary meaning of being connected does not necessarily refer to a physical, emotional, or spiritual link. Instead, the term refers to a connection to a virtual world. Our dependency on this digital connection has become powerful. While technology has incredible benefits, it also can interfere with how we establish genuine connections with the people in our lives. Studies tell us that our use of social media has led to increased anxiety, stress, exhaustion, depression, loneliness, problems with self-esteem, and even suicide. Are these maladies caused directly by our use of technology? Or are they caused by what our use of technology has sometimes displaced, which is deep, authentic relationships with our fellow human beings?

I'm not anti-tech or against social media. During my time as CEO of Chipotle, technology played a key role in better reaching and serving our customers. Overall, countless benefits have come from these technological advancements. But it is our relationships, in addition to being a powerful catalyst to a meaningful and satisfying life, that are a gateway to connecting with something even more powerful and profound. Something that exists independently of us. Like a sailboat harnesses the power of the wind, we can harness the power of this force.

Throughout my life, relationships have been the cornerstone of my own growth. They've inspired me to become a better friend, father, brother, son, businessman, author, filmmaker, public speaker, and person. Especially in leadership positions, which have allowed me the honor of leading hundreds of thousands of people, my capacity to form deep connections with others is of central importance. I wrote about this in my first book. I also created a television documentary series on PBS called *CONNECTED: A Search for Unity*, in which I explore the critical importance of interpersonal connection. Before and since writing the book and filming *CONNECTED*, I have fielded thousands of questions about how and why I developed such a unique approach to relationships. This book is my effort to answer that question.

I now see that my unusual outlook on these subjects has provided me a significant advantage in my career, as well as my spiritual growth. Improving our ability to make connections will change us. We'll be more available to others, and be better partners, spouses, parents, workers, leaders, and friends. We'll attract more wealth and abundance into our lives. We'll have more fun, feel enriched and fulfilled, and avail ourselves of profound spiritual growth. We'll look at life differently, love and be loved more deeply, and experience our lives in ways we wouldn't have thought possible.

While our modern, digital world has many advantages, the health of each of us and our society depends more than ever on balancing our virtual connectivity with authentic interpersonal connections. Without developing the skills and perspective I describe in these pages, we will lose awareness of what is most important to each of us: caring for each other and caring for our world. But if we become empowered through learning to connect more deeply, we will unlock love, power and positivity that will profoundly benefit each of us, and our world. This vision excites me greatly.

I believe the most powerful way to unleash our inner power is to become aware of what's possible for us, and of what is holding us back. Doing this will wake us up to a vision of greatness. Once awake to that vision, we won't be able to help ourselves. We will begin to powerfully elevate each other and our world.

PART I

The Power of Love

n the coming pages I ask you to make this leap of faith: that there is a force in the world you can connect with that will make your life profoundly better. This force connects us all. This connection will make life more fun, richer, and more interesting. It will make your relationships deeper and more satisfying. On top of all that, it will make you more successful in business. This force is the truth which underlies all things, and is inherently good. This idea shouldn't seem too farfetched since we often hear references to this idea in sayings such as "the truth will set you free" or "everything happens for a reason." Such sayings point to a fundamental knowledge that there is a force out there, and that the force is good. It is fair. It makes sense. It is positive and helpful.

This force is something that all of us have heard of: Love. However, as you will read throughout these pages, I have a very different way of defining love than most people. But this force called love is what underlies everything. It is everywhere, it is indestructible, and it is good. It is, as I will also discuss later, synonymous with truth and God.

I believe that seeking this connection and aligning ourselves with the power of love is the best way you can live your life: it is always the right strategy.

When I was a boy, I read somewhere the following: "whenever you feel you are about to lose something, rejoice, for what is real cannot be lost." The point of this statement is that letting go of illusions and falsity and accepting only what is real leads to a life worthy of celebration. If knowledge of the truth of this statement became widespread, there would be a lot more awareness of how we can more effectively take care of each other and our world. There would be fewer arguments and more peace. There would be less destruction of the natural world and more sensitivity to animals and plants. People would exist less in a constant state of desire for more, more, more. They'd chase fewer of the things that society tells them are important and have more bandwidth to attract the things that are most fulfilling in life: peace, fulfillment, magic, mystery, and love.

The book *The Hidden Life of Trees,* by Peter Wohlleben, tells the fascinating story of how trees are connected to one another. They communicate, warn each other, and protect each other from harm. One tool that allows them to do this is called the mycelium network, which is essentially a nervous system: a sort of fiber optic system created by millions of miles of fungal strands.

Although the mechanism for human connection is less well understood or scientifically verifiable, I believe it is no less real. We are all connected. Furthermore, I believe that most of our dysfunction as individuals and as a species results from our denial of this fundamental reality. This connection is choiceless and requires no effort. It is not a club to which we need to "opt in." Membership is automatic! Therefore, we needn't work to achieve connection with each other, or the universe: the connection is already there. However, much to our collective and individual detriment, we tend to interfere with this connection. We need to find a way to cease this interference, and set ourselves free to live spectacular and magical lives.

CHAPTER 1

What Is Love?

Love isn't what most of us think it is. We live in a world which is simultaneously obsessed with love and yet quite unaware of what love actually is. Our misunderstanding of love leads to many incorrect assumptions and decisions. As we come to better understand love, we tend to find ourselves living a much more profound, fulfilling, and interesting life.

I want to start this book with a discussion about love because I believe my perspective and understanding of love is at the heart of why my life has unfolded in a particularly magical way. You might say that my approach to love is the "magic sauce" for how I have lived my life. It's exciting to explore what this most magical and beautiful force called love is, especially since understanding love is essential for any person, organization, or country in our world.

To begin to explore what love is requires us to open our minds to looking at it very differently than most of us do now. The word is used by almost everybody, and in so many different ways, that it's valuable for us to wipe the slate clean and approach the subject afresh.

Love is so profound and so powerful and so infinite and so pervasive that there are no pithy, one-line definitions that do it justice. That is why I've dedicated a whole chapter to it.

WHAT LOVE IS NOT

Love is almost better understood by stripping away everything that it is *not*, than by jumping straight in to say what it is.

Love is not something created by human beings, and as such is not something that we control, own, or possess. Love is not like one of the elements, which exist in limited amounts, nor is it in any way constrained by the limits of the minds of living creatures. Love is not something that is created or destroyed, and so it doesn't come and go from our lives.

Being attracted to someone else because we want something they have, or something we think they can give us, isn't love. Jealousy isn't love. Possessiveness isn't love. Desiring to constrain, possess, or own isn't love—even though our society tells us that the highest expression of romantic love is to signal our possession by marrying someone.

True, when I married my wife, I really wanted her to be

"mine." I really wanted to formalize and celebrate the magical feeling we felt for each other with a ring. I said, "I love you so much I don't want you to be with anyone else." All those feelings are real. But those feelings aren't love; those are egotistical constructs. It seems sacrilegious to say that. But it's true. It has to be true, because love is not possessive and clingy and jealous.

While we may want to marry someone and have them close to us, our desire to do so isn't love. Wanting someone around more isn't love either. We might really want them around because we feel wonderful in their presence and enjoy and appreciate them —but the wanting them around is just wanting them around. It's not love. Love is something much deeper.

Because our society is almost completely ego-based (more on that later), we celebrate efforts to tie each other down as "love." We celebrate weddings with huge and lavish ceremonies, and we chalk up divorces as abject failures, even sins. But love is not created by weddings, nor ended by divorces. These are social ceremonies designed to make permanent that which cannot be made permanent. They are constructs created by the human ego to try to give us stability and permanence in an unstable and impermanent world. And while there is undoubtedly lots of love flowing at weddings, and undoubtedly a lot less love flowing during most divorces, these ceremonies do nothing to create or end love. Love is indestructible, and never goes away. Nor is it created by any human relationship. Instead, love is always there, like sunshine outside our window, waiting to drench us in its warmth, power, and acceptance.

The greatest irony of love in a romantic setting is that precisely those whom we say we "love most" are those who we tend to smother. When we feel love for someone, our ego comes running in and tries to contain them, tries to own them, tries make sure they move into the house with us and sleep with us every night. As a consequence, we often create a situation in which the person we say we love is not growing as much as they could or feeling as free as they once did. After ten years, we may look at them and say, "You're not the person I married." They might say, "You took the words right out of my mouth!" Both of us may have, probably unknowingly, erected barriers, defenses, resentments, rules, habits, coping mechanisms, and other distractions that prevent our own ability to feel the flow of love that is still all around us. We may have, inadvertently, lowered the shades, blocking out the sunlight.

Our ego was likely the driving force which led to this diminishment of what was once a beautiful connection, because our ego will naturally try to pin our partner down, and change their ways, to prevent the possibility that they'll leave us. But in the act of pinning them down and charging them with the responsibility of staying always with us and making us happy, we will have smothered them. We will have catalyzed the creation of the very defenses that limit their ability to connect and allow the very flow of love that was part of our initial attraction to them!

When we accuse them of being a different person than we married, well, we may be right! At least, they do not feel at liberty to be themselves, and thus, love isn't flowing.

To accept that many things our society calls acts of love are not love is a powerful realization, because when we know what love isn't, it generates within us a deep curiosity to know what love is. This curiosity increases our awareness and causes us to begin to better recognize and understand love. We begin to appreciate its magical power, its warm glow, its comforting presence. We begin to relax into the knowledge that love is not something created by us or eliminated by us. We relax into a place of presence and openness. We create space, and in that space love has room to rush in, surround us, and comfort us.

WHAT LOVE IS

To me, love is what's left when everything else is gone. What I mean by this is that we will feel the presence of this magnificent and magical force most powerfully when we eliminate the noise and confusion we tend to create that interferes with its natural flow. Examples of this noise and confusion are mostly ego constructs such as judgment, possessiveness, jealousy, clinging, grasping, wanting, rejecting. Bringing more love into one's life, therefore, is about making room for it, and not about working to create it or find it. It needn't be, and cannot be, earned. It isn't a product of our effort or discipline or hard work. It is an infinite and indestructible power that flows wherever there is space for it to flow.

As an analogy, imagine you are sitting quietly, alone in the woods. Seemingly out of nowhere the most beautiful humming-bird in the world flies right up to you and hovers three feet in front of your face. Your first reaction is amazement: you've never seen something so beautiful, so delicate, so magical. But then you want to capture the moment, so you reach for your phone to take a picture, and the bird flies away. Or you want to tell your friend nearby, so you yell "Oh my God, come see this," and the bird flies away. Or you try to grab the bird so you can keep it, but it flies away. It is so beautiful that you feel the need to do something, tell someone, or somehow to capture the magic of the moment. But any of these actions will cause the bird to fly away. What can you do to best enjoy this splendor and beauty? Nothing! Just watch the bird. Let it be. Remain quiet. Allow space. Anything else will end the preciousness of the moment. So it is with love. It comes when there is space for it to flow, and any grasping, desire to contain it, or effort to preserve it, will interfere with its natural flow.

Love is a force, a vibration, a light, a power. It is unlimited and omnipresent. It is infinite. It is free. It is utterly without judgment and has no preferences. It is not dependent on any-thing. It has no size, no shape, no limiting factors. It cannot be created or destroyed. It is always available, yet it does not impose itself on us if we don't want to partake of it. Love does not belong to any of us. It is not something created by people, so people cannot give it or take it, or deny someone access to it. As I will describe more fully later, I find that love is synonymous with the truth, and with God.

God. That can be a loaded word. Here's what I mean when I use the word God in this book: What if we had a word for the sum total of all that mystery, all that amazement, all the miracles that are caused by a force we cannot explain? Some people call this force God. Some people say it's a lot of science we don't understand yet. At any rate, this force, whatever it is, is infinite in its abundance. To me, this force is love, and truth, and God. One and the same.

I believe that love is the stuff of the universe: the substrate everything is built upon. Look out the window at a tree. How did it grow? It emanated from a tiny seed, and with nothing more than water and some minerality in the soil, became a tree that might weigh 100,000 pounds, and drink one hundred gallons of water a day. It seems that something massive and beautiful was created from almost nothing. From a seed that might get lost under your fingernail. When viewed in this way, a tree seems to be a miracle. The world is full of miracles like this—not just billions of trees, each one an individual miracle, but an overflowing abundance of beauty and goodness that we can try hard to explain—and it's fun to try!—but at the end of the day is too vast and mysterious to fit in the confines of our limited minds. We don't understand the universe, really. We have come up with all sorts of ways to explain it with science as well as Gods and religions and mythologies. But our understanding is still very limited.

When we human beings are able to find a moment of consciousness—when we are, for just a moment, able to see the world uncolored by our history, beyond the endless trivialities, noises and distractions of our own minds, when we are able to be present with all our faculties and can behold the brilliance of a grasshopper, a tree, a mountain, or the sky with ultimate respect, openness, curiosity, and admiration—the feeling of love arises within us.

This requires only presence and complete awareness. No effort. No desire. When we create actual mental space, we realize that we are an organism that is not separate from the grasshopper, tree, mountain, or sky. In that lack of separateness—or put differently, in our awareness of connection—a feeling of love arises. In the vacancy created by our fullest awareness, a natural curiosity arises, and love comes rushing in naturally to respond to that curiosity. We then feel a magical and powerful and satisfying connection. We are one with love.

It takes a bit of a leap of faith to accept this. You might think, "No, when everything else is gone there's nothing." But I believe love is the natural state of the universe. Many times in my life I've noticed that when I've been able to allow space, to forgive, not to label, not to be attached to anything, to release tension, to release desire, to release the noises in my mind, then I can get to a place of quiet acceptance. I always find that a positive, warm vibration fills that space. I believe that vibration is love.

As a human being, you are given the capacity to create that space and also to share it with somebody else. You can create space so that another person can feel it and partake of it. And since the power of love naturally rushes in to fill the space, others who are with you can feel it too.

The reason I believe that love works this way is partly experiential and partly logical. We know that, without any interference or action on our part, this universe came into being. It needed nothing from us. It needs nothing from us still. It is an unfathomably complex creation, yet functions in perfect balance. If we narrow our focus to the planet Earth for a moment, we can see infinite evidence of this balance. After the Earth was created, and after it cooled off enough, life of all kinds came into being. Whales and fish evolved in the seas. Animals and plants evolved on the land. Birds took to the skies. Why did all of this happen? We don't know, but we can surmise that there is a force that welcomes life. A force that invites life to partake of the abundance of this divine creation that is our home. We can see it over and over in science, in engineering, in physics, in mathematics, that the innate intelligence of our planet and all life upon it seems nearly infinite. But this intelligence is not limited to the brains of Earth's creatures. Rather, there is clearly an intelligence that belongs to the universe itself. An intelligence that predates what we call life and is not confined to any particular object or life form, and for which the source is undiscoverable through our thinking, or through science. But the source certainly exists. Something caused all of this beauty to arise. Whatever you call it, we can all agree it is real. It is true. It is this "something" that I am calling love. Or God. And this force is everywhere. This intelligence is everywhere. This is why truth is synonymous with love.

We cannot control this force. This intelligence. But we can partake of it. We can let it flow through us. We can sit in gratitude, appreciation, and awe of it. Some who read my words may simply think, "Yes. What you are describing is God!" Well, sure. I can and do easily accept that. But whether we call the force God, or whether we simply call it the power and magic of science, we can still notice that this force is, for some reason, choosing to create all this beauty. All this life. All this abundance. This infinite mystery and wonder. What is the reason? Well, I think we have to conclude that the reason is that this force is love. If the force is God, then God is love. If we want to call the force something other than God, we can still agree that the force is good, it is abundant, it is vast.

Since it is a force we do not create, it may be wrong to say we can give love to another person. But we can be a conduit of sorts, and thereby bring the energy of that love to our interactions with others. They will then sense the freshness, the power, and the warmth of that energy, and will feel naturally attracted to it. This may intimidate some who are not ready to feel it, or who are skeptical of it. But most will find it almost irresistibly attractive.

We all put out energy, and we all receive energy. The foundational energy that we exude, when we strip everything else away, is love. You may pause here and ask, "What about hate, and envy, and fear? Aren't those just as foundational?" They are not. Hate, envy, and fear are inventions of sentient beings. Mostly human beings. They are typically reactions born from our desire to survive. If you look at our universe, there is no evidence that hate, fear, or envy exist at all outside of the limited minds of some of the Earth's creatures. Yet there is infinite evidence of the intelligence that I am calling love, all around us.

An analogy might help. Think about a time when you were working quietly, and a friend came into the room and startled you. You literally jumped in fear. "Oh my God, you scared the heck out of me!" you say, and then you quickly settle down and greet your friend. Your fear was a reaction. It stemmed from a misunderstanding: you momentarily thought the sound you heard posed a threat to you. But it didn't. You were mistaken. Your fear is a response that arose from thousands of years of evolution: your ancient ancestors survived because they were startled to alertness by sounds that may have been caused by something life threatening, such as a predator. Even if nine times out of ten the thing that scared them was non-threatening, their reaction in the one dangerous circumstance saved their life. But it is fair to say that the fear that arose the other nine times was based on a misunderstanding. It was a mistake. There was no real threat. Thus, we can see that our fear, nine times out of ten, emanates from a misunderstanding. And even on the occasion where it saved our life, it was not the fear that saved us. It was the fact that we took appropriate action to run from the danger. Therefore, we can see that fear is not particularly intelligent in and of itself. The fear only got our attention. The intelligence is the decision to evade the danger. Had we felt the fear, and then done nothing, we may have been killed by the predator. What I am trying to establish by this analogy is that fear, like envy and hate, is a human construct, born out of misunderstanding. It is not a foundational aspect of universal intelligence. But love is different. Love exists independent of the animal mind.

As love begins to occupy us, we can become more trusting and comfortable with this occupation, and allow more space, and then even more love will flow through us. That's why the more love we give, the more love we have to give. When we say that someone gives us love, what is really happening is that the comfort of their loving presence allows us also to accept the love that already exists around us. This is because someone who is "loving" is not judging, is curious, is not defensive, and so we tend to let down our guard and can feel love flowing.

Love is not a finite resource. A lot of people think love is a zero-sum game—that if I love another friend, I don't have as much love for you. But love is infinite. I have no way of proving that (which is frustrating for a lawyer!), but there's a lot of circumstantial evidence, as I discussed above.

Love doesn't come from a person. Rather, love is something a person can embody. So, love isn't something that is "ours" any more than the air inside our lungs is "ours." It's not "our" air, but the distinction is irrelevant since we are free to breathe in and out. For all practical purposes there is infinite air to breathe, just as there is infinite love to flow through us.

While all of us yearn to feel the warm embrace of love, we usually prevent it from arising by crowding it out of our minds with our thoughts, such as negativity, judgment, desire, or striving. Oddly, love naturally comes into our lives when we make room for it, but it evades us when we fill our mental space by grasping for it, demanding it, or trying to manipulate our surroundings, or persuade another person to give it to us. I suppose love is most apt to be with us when we essentially get out of the way!

What I've been writing about here is something one might call "universal love." Universal love is what you get when you strip away everything else. We feel this love when we are in a state of acceptance of what is. Universal love is felt when we release our desire for things to be different. Universal love is felt when we accept the present moment—completely, without rejection. Universal love is holding sacred, with reverence and respect, something or someone in a way that allows complete connection and presence. But since I believe all love is universal love, I drop the name "universal" in most of my references throughout this book.

ROMANCE AND LOVE

There's a concept in almost all cultures, which we often hear in music and literature and other forms of art, that we need to be "worthy" of being loved. But this concept isn't true. That's not what love's about, nor is it how love operates. We can't earn love. Love isn't something we get for being worthy. It isn't something that only goes where it's deserved. It's a force that goes anywhere there is space for it to go. It flows where there is no resistance. This is consistent with what we learn in Christianity, when we're told that God's love is an act of grace. We do not earn it. We do not deserve it. It comes to us from the absolute benevolence of God. Also in Christianity, we learn that it is through faith that we are able to avail ourselves of God's love. This is very consistent with the concept of creating space in our minds. Because the process of having faith means that we essentially relax, and trust that God is with us. In that trust, that faith, our minds become quieter, stop the endless seeking, and relax. We create space. And again, love (God) naturally fills that space.

What about the feeling of being "in love?" Our culture often tells us that this feeling is what love is. Falling in love is certainly a wonderful feeling, but it's not the same thing as love.

When one is feeling "in love," they are certainly feeling love. But the love they are feeling is not actually caused by the person they are feeling "in love with." The other person isn't the source of love. Love is already around us. It is not created, nor is it destroyed. It does not come from someone else. But if that is true, why don't we always feel it? And why do we seem to feel it when we "fall in love" if it does not arise from the other person whom we are "in love with"? The answer to both of these questions is that we often erect barriers to the flow of love, which prevent us from feeling it. The main barrier that prevents us from having a constant connection to love is our ego. Our ego rejects the present moment, believing instead that our salvation lies in the future, and even then, only if things go our way: the way the ego thinks they should go. The feeling of being in love arises when our ego temporarily relaxes its grip, because it believes that a certain other person will save us from the struggles of life that the ego is always fighting against. When the ego is momentarily quieted, there is space. Love comes in to fill that space, and it feels wonderful.

Being a human being comes with many challenges and hardships. We need shelter, warmth, nutrition, clothing, and safety. We want to feel seen, valued, understood, and loved. We believe that the only way we are going to have these many things we crave is to compete and win. To be special and to fight off challenges. Then, in the midst of this ongoing struggle that the ego believes can only be won by becoming bigger, stronger, smarter, richer, prettier, and more impressive, we meet "that perfect someone" who seems, for a few precious moments, to give us hope that we can escape life's hardships, discomforts, and challenges. When we meet this person, our ego decides, for those precious moments, that it can relax its grasping and clawing and competing. It believes that if we can just pin down this one perfect someone, they'll deliver us from all the darkness, fear, and discomfort. So we relax into them. We trust them. We believe in them. We say we love only them. It is so juicy and romantic, this feeling. We basically feel that the rest of the world can go away. We finally found our precious someone. During this time, we accept the moment and are present, our ego goes dormant, and there is space. Love, as it always does, rushes in to fill that space.

But, of course, in time we learn that even our special love interest cannot keep the hardships of life from rearing their head. When we learn this, we feel crestfallen. Maybe even betrayed! We find that our special person cannot do for us what we thought they could, and we are gravely disappointed. At that point, we may come to resent our special person, or even believe that they are not so special after all. We decide that we have made a mistake, and that maybe we should move on to look once again for that "perfect someone." If our ego remains our primary guide, that is exactly what we will do. We will move on. But if we can grow enough to realize that eliminating life's hardships is not possible (nor even desirable), and that it is no one's duty to provide us access to the warm feeling of love, then we may decide that our special person really is worthy of our continued loyalty and interest. This is when a longer, deeper, and more spiritually enriching relationship has a chance to develop.

When we are newly in love we almost can't help but think, "This is what love feels like." We're not entirely wrong, because being "in love" can momentarily satisfy the ego, and with its release, temporarily bring us in touch with the love that exists all around us. When we fall in love, we feel that the other person loves us, cares about us, and will do anything to make us happy. We feel seen, valued, understood, and loved, and the experience of the moment feels like a permanent state. We think, "Finally!"

Yet love is different than "being in love." Being in love arises from a brief cessation of the rejection of the present moment caused by our ego. It's similar to the feeling of triumph a climber feels on the summit of Everest. For a moment, he feels like "I did it, this is it!" But the moment is only fleeting. The climber has to descend Everest after his moment of triumph, and the person who is "in love" has to return to the reality that life, even with this new, exciting person in it, is full of struggle, pain, doubt, and hardship. Therefore, feeling in love does not give us sustainable access to the feeling and power of love.

LOVE IS EASY

The human being is a very industrious animal. We are always thinking, trying to solve problems, and working to improve, grow, and become something more. The irony is that, through this striving, we sometimes lose our way. Because if we are honest, most of our striving and hard work is an effort to feel seen, valued, understood, and loved.

As adults, we famously look for love in the material world. We believe love will come to us when we are wealthy, or powerful, or when we get the right partner, the right home, or live in the right neighborhood with the right friends. In other words, we feel that love is something to be earned through effort, toil, struggle, and hard work. But all of this effort is irrelevant to whether we experience love. In fact, I've noticed that the wealthiest people often have a harder time finding love in their lives, because the allure of material wealth has them chasing things that are more supportive of a growing ego, and less supportive of creating the kind of vulnerability and space that will invite love into their lives.

To the extent there is any relationship between materialism and love it is often an inversely proportional one. That is, the more material objects we chase, the less likely we are to allow space for love. To the extent there is any relationship between effort and love, it is likewise often an inversely proportional one.

Paradoxically, rather than wealth leading to love (which it doesn't do), it is a truer statement that welcoming more love into your life tends to lead to more wealth. By allowing love to flow into our lives, we will attract more abundance into our lives. This is true because when we are striving to satisfy the insatiable ego we are essentially swimming against the current. We are wasting a lot of time and energy chasing things that do not provide satisfaction or contentment, which leaves us frustrated. In our frustration, we tend to work even harder to fulfill the endless desires of the ego. But if we realize that love exists only in the present moment, and that we will feel it only if we open our hearts and create space for it, we are swimming with the current. Then whatever we are engaged in, we will bring our full attention and skill to it. We will do better work, give better service, create a better product, and so forth.

The game of golf might provide a useful analogy here. Golf is simultaneously the most fun and most frustrating game I've ever played. It turns out that the way to hit the ball best, furthest, and most accurately is to swing in a smooth, relaxed way. If you put in too much effort, or try to swing too hard, the result is almost always a terrible shot. It doesn't go as far, and it usually goes the wrong direction. But when one trusts that the golf club will do the work, and just relaxes and swings nice and easy, the ball flies far and accurately, producing a wonderful warm fuzzy feeling that makes you feel, for a moment, like a pro. So why is the game so difficult? Because it is human nature to believe, deep in your soul, that more effort is better. That hitting it harder is better. It is so difficult to teach your body, and your mind, to relax. It is, for me, often close to impossible. I keep thinking if I try harder, swing harder, put some muscle into it, I'll do better. But once again, I hit the ball terribly, and often lose my ball! On the rare occasions when I just relax, I can hit lovely shots. It is so counterintuitive that less effort, less strain, less muscle, will produce a longer shot. But that is exactly what it takes to be great at golf. The pros make it look so easy.

Like a great golf shot, the love we crave, that we try so fervently to earn, is already there waiting for us, if we can relax and allow it. If we can trust that it is there. Like the sunlight that flows naturally in the window when we open the shade, we can likewise relax and allow love to flow.

Love is easy. It is not difficult. This is why time in nature is so precious and helpful to us in returning to the simple, fresh, easy, and open connection we have with the power and glory of the love that surrounds us. As the sun sets, and as geese fly overhead with their rhythmic song, and as a gentle breeze blows my hair as I write this, I am reminded how simple it all really is. Love arises more from allowing than it does from doing. More from openness than effort. More from gentle awareness than searching.

When we begin to talk about love in the context of relationship, it is important to bear in mind that it is the same love I've already described. When we are truly in touch with love and allowing it to flow into us and through us, we will feel love for whoever we are with. We won't just love certain people and not love others. Because love does not discriminate.

I expect you think I am wrong about this. Let me explain. The reason we are able to feel love for some people, and we are not able to feel love for others, has more to do with the state of our minds than it has to do with the actual presence or absence of love. We will feel love for someone when we allow space to exist with them. This space arises from vulnerability. It arises from relaxing. From trusting. From being open to what arises. From releasing judgment, which crowds out the energy of love. When we bring this state of mind to another, and they bring it to us, we will feel love for them, and they for us, no matter if they are a man or woman, thin or fat, or even if we speak the same language. If any two people are curating space in themselves which allows for the presence of love, they will feel a warm and trusting association with the other. They will feel love.

This way of thinking stands in stark contrast with our ego-based and incorrect understanding of love as only existing when we meet that someone special. What is hugely ironic is that it seems somehow unromantic to think that there is more than one person we can love. But why would we find that unromantic? Isn't more love more romantic than less love? Isn't such an assumption like thinking one gold nugget superior to an endless pile of riches? At any rate, the truth is, when we are filled with love (which happens when we create the space for it to flow through us) it is impossible not to love another person. Again, love is not a discriminating force.

But why then do we tend to think we love certain people, and not love others? Why do we marry "that certain someone"? Why do we celebrate that our friend "finally found that special someone to love"? The beginning of the answer is that we are afraid to love everyone. Loving everyone requires absolute vulnerability, openness to, and trust for all of mankind. We are afraid that if we do this, we will appear weak and be taken advantage of. We are afraid our openness will lead to betrayal and heartbreak.

In truth, it might. The Christians describe how Jesus loved everyone, without regard to their status, wealth, work ethic, race, or deeds. The result was that most of the Roman world misunderstood him, were threatened by him, and their leaders crucified him. It is not too surprising that we mere mortals may be hesitant to open our hearts completely to the world around us. After all, the world is rife with examples of people who take advantage, act from their ego, seek power and material wealth over love, and harm others in their effort to make themselves bigger and stronger. I am not advocating that any of us walk naively through life with our guard completely down. But I am advocating that we at least understand the true nature of love, which is that it does not harbor preferences, it does not discriminate, it does not love some and hate others. If we remain aware of this, we will be able to live more skillfully and with more fulfillment.

Loving someone means allowing the love that occupies you to flow to them and allowing the love that occupies them to flow to you. It means you are bringing total vulnerability to the present moment and celebrating their willingness to do the same. This can happen almost instantly in an encounter with a stranger walking down the street, or a person who is sitting next to you on an airplane flight or a bus. Let's not concern ourselves that the feeling you have in these situations is somehow not real love. It is love. But it is important to understand that the love that you are feeling comes from your willingness to allow it to arise, not from the other person. Indeed, the very fact that the aforementioned relationships are made safe by their temporary nature is exactly what allows us to feel love within them. We are open, and we are vulnerable, because there is no real risk. If it starts to feel bad, unsafe, untrusting, or uncomfortable, we can walk away!

When loving someone leads to a longer-term romantic involvement, then it entails a commitment to maintaining that openness and vulnerability with another person on a long-term basis. This is much more difficult to do, because as we spend more time together, life happens! Each of us has an ego, and our egos are not trusting, are never satisfied, and will quickly make efforts to pin our new love interest down. As I write about in Chapter 4, our egos are afraid. They want to ensure that things remain as they are when it is the very nature of the universe that they will not remain as they are. We start to feel a lack of trust, a desire to possess the other person, or a desire that the other person become someone they are not. As challenging circumstances arise, as we see our partner is a little too delighted to be talking to that good looking guy over there, or as our partner refuses to do the dishes, we begin to judge. Resentment arises. We may feel unseen. We may feel threatened. Those feelings fill the space in our minds that needs to remain available in order for love to continue to flow. So our egos are engaged, the warm feeling of love is displaced, and the relationship becomes a challenge.

The concept of ego is very important to a better understanding of love, which is why you'll find a much deeper discussion of it in a few pages.

All that being said, I believe in marriage. I think it is beautiful. The reason it is beautiful is that for a marriage to be successful, one needs to work through one's issues, accept realities that may be very uncomfortable, and come to grips with change. All of this entails real spiritual growth. In fact, I believe such long-term relationships are an excellent crucible for spiritual growth.

This growth entails the deepening of one's understanding of reality. Since reality is good and true and based on the power of love, a marriage can powerfully deepen one's personal development and growth towards a more profound connection with the truth, love, and God. The very commitment to work through tough times with a partner is a worthy and noble goal. It brings a sacred depth to the relationship. It allows us to practice developing our vulnerability, openness, and acceptance. This is an incredibly worthwhile path for us to navigate because these lessons bring us a deeper understanding of the truth about ourselves, and about others. In a marriage, by learning to trust that love will persist in our relationship even as we change, grow, and learn, we learn to trust more deeply in the very love that sits as the foundation of the universe.

Because love and truth are synonymous, loving someone means feeling a deep and authentic connection with the reality of another person's being. Fostering such connections serves to help us deepen our own feeling of connectedness with the universal consciousness that many call God. In other words, relationships with people can be a catalyst for our own connection with truth, love, and God. This means that relationships are both important and sacred. Making connections with others requires us to let go of our defenses, relax, open our hearts, and experience the natural flow of the love that exists all around us. When we're able to have this experience in the presence of another person, such that we feel the endless grace and beauty of love, we tend to say that we love the person we are with. But again, the love we are feeling does not belong to us, nor does it originate from the other person: instead, it exists as the background reality which surrounds us at all times.

The trust, openness, and surrender we allow in the presence of certain other people enables us to accept, become one with, and experience some part of the infinite love that exists all around us.

When we first start to define love in the way I am discussing, it may seem rather unromantic. After all, there is something profoundly warm and comforting about the notion that there is one special person in the world who is our soul mate. Or that there is one person that is our best friend. But the specialness that we feel when we label someone as being in one of these roles with us is real. We are capable of appreciating someone's uniqueness, and that leads us to feel gratitude for them, and warmth towards them, which increases our connection with them. There is nothing unromantic about that. In fact, I would argue that wanting to be with someone not because you feel you need them to feel love, but because their unique presence helps you to have a closer relationship with the truth, love and God is incredibly romantic!

Within a relationship, we can hold someone else in our care and attention, be curious about them, and honor and respect their complexity, history and their being. When we bring presence and compassion to another person in this way, that is love. When we allow this, love is a desire to honor that person by doing nothing to inhibit their growth. We are there for them, and if at some time we can do something for them, we consider it an honor.

You may ask yourself, after reading all this, "Gee, are any of us really capable of love?"

We are not able to love someone at the most idealized level as long as our ego is in charge. When our ego is dictating our actions, we will see other people in terms of what we can get from them, rather than in terms of how we can develop a connection based on mutual care and support. Loving without allowing our ego to dominate is like finding a piece of gold in a river, admiring it, and then putting it back. You know it is there, but you needn't claim it is yours. Instead, your appreciation comes from feeling in your heart your capacity to love it, to see it, to admire it, but not to limit it, own it, keep it, or pin it down. When we can learn to understand this kind of love and start to view our relationships with others in this light, we can begin to live our lives in a more skillful way: a way that allows us to hold sacred the connections that bring us closer to the truth that is love and is God. To allow them to be, and not label them as ours. To relax our egoic clinging and desires, and rest into a trusting relationship with love. To be present with and feel our deepest connection and gratitude for the people and world around us. This is the most powerful way to live our lives. Perhaps surprisingly, it isn't grasping or yearning, but the release of our desire for more, and finding gratitude for the moment we are living in now, that attracts more beauty, abundance, and goodness into our lives.

Welcoming the flow of love is always the best strategy for living our lives. If we understand what love truly is, and welcome it into our lives, we will live a far more enriching, satisfying, and fulfilling life. We will stop using others, extracting from them, taking from them. Instead, we will treat them with reverence and respect. This will dramatically improve our ability to connect with others, and strengthen our relationships. People will feel the generosity of our heart, and they will be drawn to us, since we will become a source of enrichment for them. We will be seen as strong by others, and they will respect us, and our opinions will be given greater weight. We will find ourselves in leadership positions because our behavior will empower others to be at their best. This is the most powerful formula for success in any life, business, or organization.

We will begin to take responsibility for ourselves and will stop blaming others for things we are dissatisfied with. We will no longer feel like, or claim to be, victims. We will have the power to guide our lives with more power and clarity in a brilliant union with the truth, love, and God.

We will stop using others as building blocks for our continued ego development, and instead will see them as someone with whom to share a connection. We will have compassion for our ego and see it for what it is: a mechanism that has been trying to protect us, but which also dramatically interferes with our spiritual awakening. We may then gain some independence from our ego. This means we won't need to use others to build our self-esteem, which will free us to rejoice in their growth, their development, and awakening. This means we can see others and appreciate them for who they are, and love them. A natural outflow of this love will be that we will treat others with care, and we will help others blossom into the fullest versions of themselves. We will be a light in the world. A source of goodness and positivity. A source of peace and harmony. Someone better capable of bringing to society the solutions that will make the world a better place.

All of these incredibly valuable gifts, these profound advantages, await us when we open our hearts, relax our egos, and embrace the power of love as the guide for our lives.

THIS IS ALL A GIFT

The world we live in is a fantastically complex place. Living within this world as a human being, which is one of the most complex life forms on the planet, only adds to the complexity. That is to say, life is and should be difficult. We are creatures with hundreds of billions of nerve cells designed to help us experience and survive in the world. But despite this complexity and associated difficulty, the experience of life on Earth is something good and worthy, even brilliant, sacred, wonderful, and beautiful. Our experience here is a gift, and it is a gift that allows us to draw nearer and nearer to understanding the actual truth of the universe. I believe that the closer you get to that truth, the closer you get to God. Being close to God is the key to experiencing contentment and fulfillment. Fulfillment does not mean there is no further pain or sadness. Instead, it means acceptance and appreciation, without rejection, for the gift of life. We will still experience pain, but we will not suffer or complain about it. We will still feel sadness, but we will not suffer or complain about it. We will still have hardships, but we will take them in stride, with grace and skill.

If you want to develop a close relationship with the truth, you have to accept the deep complexity of human existence, which includes things like aging, pain, frustration, anxiety, and other unpleasant sensations. Of course, you will also have pleasant sensations, moments of feeling refreshed and alive and awake and in touch. You sometimes will feel daft and confused and silly, sometimes sick and feverish. All of those feelings are part of the human experience. No human being can escape them—not Jesus Christ, not Buddha, not anyone. This is true precisely because the human experience places us in a body that is exposed to the many physical challenges of the universe. But there is huge value in that struggle.

That is, I believe, why we are here! To struggle. To learn. To grow, blossom and develop. And then, after much learning, to die. But even that death is part of the growth process, because at death, we merge with and into the universal consciousness, which is love, and is God.

CHAPTER 2

Waking Up

In February of 2015, at the invitation of my dear friends Doug Coe and Ariuna Namsrai, I had the opportunity to meet with His Holiness, the Fourteenth Dalai Lama, in a hotel in Washington DC. I was excited to meet him, as I had seen interviews of him over the years, read some quotes, and always found him to be wise yet light and funny. He was, I thought, likely one of the world's most spiritually awakened people. Having a strong interest in Eastern philosophy, and a warm feeling for the man I believed him to be, I couldn't imagine anyone I'd rather meet.

As I waited in a lobby in the Washington Hilton, Doug emerged from an adjacent room and motioned for me. I quietly walked into a large conference room, simply arranged with a few chairs, where only His Holiness stood.

As I approached the Dalai Lama, he stood still, clad in his monk's robe, a wonderful smile calmly resting on his lips, his hand outstretched towards me. Doug introduced me, "Your Holiness, this is Monty Moran. Monty is a businessman who works to help underprivileged people attain leadership positions." As Doug continued with more complimentary words about my career, it sounded like Doug was giving the Dalai Lama my resume, which I sensed was irrelevant to the monk who stood before me. I reached out my hand: "It's an honor to meet you," I said. As I said this, he took my hand gently in both of his.

At this point, normally people would shake hands, but the notion of shaking hands suddenly seemed silly. In a flash, I realized that the reason people shake hands is to prevent the physical contact of handholding from feeling overly intimate. This warm and beautiful monk and I held hands for a minute or so, looking quietly at each other. We remained like this until he asked me to take a seat in the large chair next to him. There were ten chairs in a big horseshoe shape, four simple chairs on each side of the horseshoe and two throne-like chairs at the base of the horseshoe. He selected one of the less comfortable chairs for himself and guided me into a chair of greater prominence and comfort. While my mind noticed that taking a fancier chair seemed backward, my heart instantly felt completely comfortable accepting his generous invitation. I spoke with him for several minutes, and the conversation was as warm and comfortable as a conversation with an old friend, yet also fresh and new. It was clear that the words themselves were not what was most profound. Instead, the specialness came from a deep connection and presence that I felt between us.

We were both fully together, completely undistracted by anything else, and smiling radiantly at each other. I felt an unmistakable feeling between us. It was in the air all around, just like the lovely smell of a flower lingers throughout a garden. A feeling of warmth, togetherness, stillness, acceptance, and understanding. It was unmistakable. The feeling was love.

I soon heard the sounds of the other people entering the room, and they approached His Holiness. I tried to stand and leave but the Dalai Lama, with the gentlest raising of his hand, motioned for me to stay where I was.

As the others approached, I could still feel the warm feeling of connection lingering between us. As they walked up, each of them shook his hand, and each said a number of words designed to justify why they were worthy of the meeting—what made them an important person. They said things like, "Your holiness, I am CEO of XX company, and we are involved with giving money to support children in Tibet. I'm even studying the Tibetan language!" There wasn't a single one of these people who didn't offer a resume of accomplishments to this quiet monk, who, at the close of their words, simply looked at each and said, "Oh! I see!" or "Ah, OK. Thank you."

I noticed how these people seemed to feel the need to prove themselves deserving of this meeting by virtue of their worldly accomplishments. This seemed painfully out of touch with what was going on in the room. At any rate, soon the line of executives completed their introductions to the Dalai Lama. Some sat in chairs. Others remained standing.

Doug asked His Holiness to make some remarks, which he did. But as he started to make his remarks, he turned toward me, softly took my hand again, and looked deeply in my eyes. I felt momentarily self-conscious that his posture was directed so uniquely toward me. But as he held my hand, I relaxed. He was funny. Warm, friendly, and familiar, as though I'd known him my whole life. I felt that nothing could feel more normal than sitting here talking to him. It was completely ordinary and comfortable.

What made the experience stand out in my mind was how regular and completely normal it was to be with this man. That is, what made it extraordinary was exactly that it was so ordinary. You might say that it was "extra-ordinary." Extraordinary for the very reason that it was just so perfectly real, simple, genuine, present, and loving. No pretenses. No awkward formalities. No rules. No judging people on their achievements or accomplishments. No ego. He was a wonderfully open-hearted, warm, wise, and relaxed monk, and it felt light and safe and warm to just hold his hand and spend some wonderful time together.

I found in the Dalai Lama a complete and loving human being: totally present, and with a heart that was completely available. His presence gave rise to space: a kind of lightness in which understanding, warmth, trust, comfort, and love seemed to arise around him. People seek him out for this. They want to follow him because of his immense capacity to truly love and understand and care for the people around him. He has become a powerful leader.

I think the Dalai Lama offers a wonderful example as to how to live our most fulfilling life.

We have a choice as to how to live our lives. If we live in a "spiritually awakened state," we live in the present, confront each experience as something new and fresh, and find life mysterious and interesting. Or we can live a life where we are spiritually asleep, where past experiences and apprehension about the future dominate our consciousness, leading us to react to and judge every person and experience, unable to see the truth of each moment as it arises. The latter allows little room for love to arise. To me, that's not really living. We become like a machine, simply reacting to inputs. Our life is not fresh. It's not new. It's not interesting. Reacting doesn't allow us to chart our own path. It doesn't allow us to grow and blossom into our fullest self. We become like the dreaming creatures in *The Matrix*, a movie premised on the idea that humans are enslaved by machines that harness their energy and deny their humanity, kept in a dream state that makes them think they are free. You can dream a nice dream, but you're missing out on connection with others and connection with the universe.

WHAT IS WAKING UP?

Particularly at a young age, many people are looking mostly for an exciting, busy, eventful, and fast-paced life, and think that spirituality is for someone else. Or just for groovy people. Maybe even unnecessary and boring! The vast majority of people will likely take little time during their lives to consider their spiritual development. And so, for many, life becomes an ever-unfolding struggle in which they have an ongoing series of desires or goals and set about trying to accomplish them, without any real thought about what it means to awaken. For others, though, something happens that stimulates a desire to live a deeper, more meaningful life.

I count myself lucky, for the question of what it means to be spiritually awake and why this matters is one I have considered throughout my life. For me, the hunger to awaken hatched early, when I noticed that I was unfulfilled by the very things that society had insisted were important.

I began to notice that I didn't really care who won the football game.

I noticed that the money I earned from years of hard work wasn't as gratifying as the satisfaction I got from simply doing the work.

I noticed that many rich and famous people were often not very happy, while some of the poorest people I met had great wisdom to share, the greatest capacity for appreciation, and were the most interesting to hang out with.

I began to see a depth of absurdity in the way human beings thought, behaved, worked, fought, and competed.

I noticed that the things that mattered most to me were often not given much attention by my teachers or society's leaders.

In all my years of school, there was no class on:

- How to grow to become a good and honorable person.
- How to best love, care for, and relate to each other.
- How to lead to a life of well-being and fulfillment.
- How all life on Earth is essential, beautiful, and sacred.
- How to have excellent relationships.
- How to empower the people around us to be at their best, and why this is the best way to lead our lives.
- How to avoid becoming trapped in the habit of seeking things that are not lastingly fulfilling.
- How material objects do not tend to bring us happiness or fulfillment.
- How the natural world, and all species which live on it, live in a delicate and harmonious balance.

As a young person, I started to wonder about these questions. I found the answers to be more important than most of what I was learning. That made me wonder about the human race. We tell ourselves we are the smartest creatures to ever walk the Earth, yet we do not teach our young the most important things! Instead, we generally teach kids to go out and compete in society for wealth and power. Is that really as important as the other topics above? Even if it is, why not teach the other stuff too?

WHAT DOES IT MEAN TO BE AWAKE?

Some people become attracted to spiritual work because they suffer from a lot of psychological pain, and they believe that their salvation lies in spirituality and a deeper connection with God or the universe. Other people become attracted to spirituality because their ego tells them that they can become superior to others if they become enlightened. (Of course, this path just leads to an ever-increasingly powerful ego and will not be effective.) No matter what draws one to begin an inquiry into waking up, the journey is an interesting and exciting one.

But what does it even mean to be spiritually awake?

To me, being awake means having a deep comprehension of and a healthy relationship with reality such that we live in a state of peaceful awareness, gratitude, harmony, acceptance and connection with the truth. While we are aware of our past experiences, we are able to live fully in the moment, without allowing our past to interfere with the fullness of our present experience. We can observe and appreciate things as they are, without mentally labeling them or applying our biases in such a way as to limit our perceptions. We are able to accept challenges as they confront us, and embrace them with skill, and without rejection or negativity.

Being awake means our ego is not dictating our thoughts or actions, which means we have more mental space, allowing us to be more attuned to the sensory world around us. This mental space, which is free of thought, allows us to be guided not by egoic dysfunction, but instead by the wisdom, power and love that exist in the world around us. When we are awake, we become psychologically light and feel fresh, freed from the burden of judgment, negativity, guilt, desire, the weight of our past, or concerns of our future. Being awake means we are present in the moment. We feel a reverence, and sense of awe and connection to the universe. We feel lifted by a power and presence that has the flavor of gratitude, confidence, optimism, radiance, and knowledge that things are as they should be. When we are spiritually awake, our mind is still and quiet, even if our external circumstances aren't.

Being in the presence of His Holiness the Dalai Lama, I felt that he lived his life in an awakened state, which made being with him feel fresh, light, and healthy. He seemed unburdened. This made it wonderful to spend time with him. Most of us seldom exist in an awakened state. Instead, we find ourselves in a state of near constant dissatisfaction. We feel sensations and feelings that we'd prefer not to have and we desire things or feelings that we don't have. The Buddhists say that all suffering is caused by exactly this: the desire to have what we don't have, or to not have what we do have.

Being awake does not mean having some kind of externally perfect life. The human condition is complex and filled with moments of discomfort and pain. Being awake does not mean eliminating these discomforts. It means accepting them. When we are spiritually awake, we still will have moments of pain and discomfort. But we will no longer reject them or spend energy wishing things were different. Instead, we will accept each moment as it arises, trusting and knowing it to be the right moment for us.

Christians do not typically talk in terms of spiritual awakening, but I believe that the aim of Christian faith is much the same as what I've outlined above. Christians seek a state of mental well-being through their faith. They say that if we have faith that Jesus died for our sins, and if we accept Jesus as our lord and savior and ask for the forgiveness of our sins, we are thereby reborn to a life everlasting and accepted into the kingdom of heaven. This faith allows Christians to forgive themselves as Jesus forgives them, which essentially means they can once again live in harmony with the present moment. God's forgiveness removes their burdens, such that they find inner peace and tranquility, even in difficult life circumstances.

If we really consider the Buddhist view, the Christian view, or the view that I describe wherein we connect with the universal love that surrounds us, we can see that these views are not inconsistent. They all end up in the same place. The idea in each case is that, in order to realize an awakened state (which the Christians might call salvation or life everlasting, and which the Buddhists might call awakeness or enlightenment), we let go of our rejections, judgments, longings, desires, and clinging, to arrive at a place of complete acceptance of what is. We embrace the present moment as being what we need at this time. We bring gratitude to this moment. We say "yes" to our experience now. Only by doing so do we become our fullest selves. In such moments we will notice that we are not suffering, but instead are at peace. We may feel pain and discomfort, but we won't suffer. In other words, there will not be negative mental commentary accompanying any physically unpleasant sensations.

Awakening has more to do with letting go than it has to do with obtaining something. Literally, we become less to become more. We release our endless grasping and clinging and wanting and needing, so that we can become truly alive and one with something much greater.

When we are awake, we do not add drama. We do not bring our history or negative mental labels to our current situation. We do not label what is happening now as good or bad, but instead see the freshness and newness of this moment as sacred and unique.

Most people live with a near constant desire that things be different. This is their normal state of being. A constant state of dissatisfaction. This is the function of the ego, which I discuss in depth in Chapter 4. Most people spend their time thinking about how they can change their life to be something more worthwhile, more exciting, more enriching. The problem is that this constant desire for things to be other than as they are prevents us from appreciating the reality of our lives. We will not ever find satisfaction or contentment in rejection and dissatisfaction. Our constant effort to change our external circumstances unfortunately won't provide the satisfaction we seek. Rather, it is exactly these efforts that perpetuate the dissatisfaction.

The key to waking up is to begin to become aware of this. To watch ourselves and begin to see the silliness of rejecting what is. To begin to see that this moment is all we have, and that the future is not the source of redemption from our dissatisfaction. In fact, the future cannot offer us anything since it is not even real, only an abstract mental concept in our own minds. If we want true satisfaction, the thing that delivers it must be real. If it is merely a fantasy or a figment of our imagination, which the future obviously is, then it cannot offer us joy or satisfaction. The only thing that is real is this moment. It is the only thing that is. If we can bring our awareness, gratitude, and focus to this moment, we can begin to feel the warm feeling of being awake. Of having arrived home. Of being one with the reality of the universe, which is love, and is truth, and is God.

To be present, nothing is required but our full awareness. Our full attention. There is nothing that needs to be solved. It is in this moment where we feel alive. In fact, it's the only time we are alive! It's where we have access to truth and wisdom that is not limited by the confines of our human existence. When we're totally present, we reach a higher level of consciousness that is not "ours," yet we are fully able to participate in that consciousness.

WAKING UP TO THE PRESENT

Waking up is exhilarating and exciting. How do I know this? Well, to be honest, because I have spent a lot of time in the realm of ego, rejecting myself and my life. I have spent a lot of time suffering. But through my practice, I began to observe when I was present, and when I was not. I started to notice when I was overtaken by the seductive power of my ego, and when I was free of my ego, and embracing the present moment. Over time, I have grown more able to remain in a state of connection to reality, which has allowed me to see, love, and appreciate our world and the people in it much more profoundly. Am I enlightened? No. I'm not. That would mean living perpetually in a state of absolute presence and egolessness, and that is not my current experience. But I do notice, as I grow, I spend more time awake and aware. More time in the present. More time where I'm truly available to connect with others. More time feeling the warm glow of love inhabiting my heart.

On the path to waking up, we tend to see more of the absurdity in certain things, like the way our society behaves. Life gets lighter. We don't feel so heavy and serious. We may start to see aspects of the human condition as funny. We may find ourselves giggling, when we are all alone, at the simplest observations. We start to feel more compassion for others and a desire to help them to avail themselves of the present moment. We may feel a little sad, too, as we notice the cost to others, and the world around us, of a vast population of human beings who largely remain spiritually asleep.

There's great comfort in the present moment. There is complete awareness. You notice sounds. You notice birds chirping. You become more attuned. Your nervous system aligns and settles. It's as if you are an excellent antenna for all that exists in the world. You notice stress you have been carrying, that you'd been unaware of. You realize you are worried about things that may or may not happen, for which worrying does no good and solves nothing. As you drop further into the present you feel a sense of confidence that as new situations arise you have the capacity to address them intelligently and not reactively, with wisdom, instead of old, egoic, unskilled habits.

You may feel a sense of calm in the face of things or events that previously bothered you. For example, I recently received a text from a man who I used to do business with. It was the first text I had received from him in over two years. Previously he had been very complimentary, even telling me that he loved me. But this text said,

"Heya. I forgive you. I don't like you. And. I forgive you."

This man and I had had a fair amount of history together. In fact, I had bought his company three years before. At the moment I read this text, I was quite present. Quite awake. As I read it, I noticed that it did not hurt my feelings. I realized that it was likely that, even though he initially felt very grateful when I bought his company, he may feel resentful about it now. At any rate, the mere fact that this message did not hurt my feelings was a major change from how I would have reacted years before. I would have panicked at the thought of someone not liking me, and I would've scrambled to call him and find out what was going on. But in this case, I realized he was likely going through a hard time and feeling angry. I also realized that I did like him, despite what he might be feeling about me. I responded:

"Well, I do like you. I send you my best wishes."

Immediately, he replied, "Love ya."

In my relatively awakened state, I was able to allow the reality of the moment without rejection, without mental complaint, without fear. In fact, his message that he did not like me actually warmed me, because I felt honored that he felt so willing to share these difficult feelings with me. His feeling of not liking me was real. It was how he was feeling, and he took the time to share it with me. My mind relaxed, accepted it, and felt gratitude for his message.

On the path of awakening, you will notice that the way you respond to the outside world begins to change. You begin to notice you're less reactive to external stimuli that used to trigger a strong reaction. You may find you experience the world in a more nuanced way: you'll have more mental space to observe how things are and will interject fewer of your own judgments. This allows your experience of the reality of the present moment to broaden. For example, you may find points of view which differ from your own to be more tolerable. You will see others with more compassion.

On this path, you may develop a sense of peace, because there is more mental space than you are accustomed to. While you may tend towards quickly filling that space (the ego hates space—it is boring, uncomfortable, and even threatening to the ego), on other occasions you may experience that space without trying to fill it right away. It is in that space that wakefulness exists.

As I wrote in my first book, *Love Is Free, Guac Is Extra*, I believe that the natural state of human beings is to blossom, develop and grow. Just as a flower naturally grows toward sunlight, a human being's natural state is to grow toward a higher level of consciousness, understanding and truth. If, for a time, a human being does not grow, it's because dysfunction is present.

It's as if you took a seed and placed it beneath a giant rock. The seed might sprout and grow, but it would have to find its way around that rock before it could reach the sunlight and go on to become a fully realized tree. It's not bad to grow that way, because growth is growth, and I believe that's human nature. Someone who chooses not to grow is denying their essential human nature, just as a seed that chose not to grow (if a seed could choose) would deny its essential nature.

WAKING UP & CONNECTION

One reason spiritual growth is so enriching is that it is essential to maximize our capacity to form deep and authentic relationships with others. And as I said in the introduction, the quality of your relationships determines the quality of your life.

Relationships between people who are still primarily operating from their ego are not lastingly fulfilling. This is true because, when both people are operating from ego, they are not fully seeing each other and therefore cannot fully relate to each other. If you remain spiritually asleep, that is, in a mental state dominated by ego and compulsive thinking, your relationships will lack depth and authenticity. You won't be able to bring your most powerful self to help others. This would be a shame, since the world stands to greatly benefit from your brilliance.

It's worth waking up because when we are able to be in the present, which is the same thing as being awake, we access God.

We access truth. We access brilliance. We access love. We access reality. We access freshness. We access a deeper connection with everyone and everything.

When we are aware and are present we apply ourselves much more intelligently to our lives. We live more skillfully. We see others for who they are. We can even see when a person is acting from a place of ego and allow it, but not feel the need to punish or dislike them, or to generate any negativity.

CHAPTER 3

Essential Connection Tools: Vulnerability and Curiosity

As a young a lawyer in Denver during the 1990s, I quickly developed a close professional relationship with one of the founders of the firm. He was a big, strong, former Army Ranger. In other words, he was intimidating as hell. But I was doing good work, he saw that, and he started to ask my opinion about a lot of things.

One day he and I had an argument about something pretty unimportant, but somehow it caused him to snap. I was challenging his viewpoint on something, and suddenly he got furious. He slammed the glass of water he'd been drinking down on the desk, splashing water on me, and yelled at me.

I didn't say anything. I felt startled, threatened, and afraid. I no longer felt I was in a mental state where I could skillfully interact with him. I calmly got up and walked out, even as he called after me to come back. I went back to my office and closed the door.

I had not been at the firm a year. I was on track to make partner. But I was very sensitive to being yelled at. I felt pain and fear and shock. A few minutes later he came into my office.

"Why didn't you come back when I called you?" he asked.

I looked up at him, saw that his temper had cooled, and heard that he had softened in his tone. I could feel, once again, that my heart could begin to open back up to him. But I remained hurt, and I didn't want to allow what had happened to stand without discussion. With tears in my eyes, I calmly and slowly said, "It hurt my feelings when you slammed your glass down and yelled at me. I am a sensitive person, and I don't want to be around people who treat me like that. After experiencing that, I'm even wondering if this firm is the right one for me."

At that moment, to my surprise, this big, frightening man who seemed as unwavering and impermeable as a stone fortress began to tear up. "Monty, I want to tell you something. I look at you both as the little brother I never had, and my best friend," he said. "I can see how much I hurt your feelings, and I will never yell at you like that again. I'm really sorry."

He never did.

I stayed with the firm another ten years. I soon became the CEO. This man and I became very close. We were aligned about how to run the business, and the firm was very successful. Had he not yelled at me like that, and had I not had the opportunity to tell him how much it hurt, I'm not sure that we would ever have become as close as we did. It is not that being hurt was necessary. What was necessary was for us to achieve the level of vulnerability we shared. That allowed us to find a new depth of connection. This difficult interaction, which led to my expressing my feelings to him, allowed us both to go to a deeper place because we each shared a vulnerability that we otherwise wouldn't have shared.

WHAT IS VULNERABILITY?

Deep personal connections arise only from a place of vulnerability. And that begs the question: what is vulnerability?

Vulnerability is a state of openness wherein we are able to allow ourselves to be totally present without defensiveness. It is a state of trust and receptivity. We let down our guard and open ourselves to experience what arises, without defense, resistance, or rejection. We trust that we belong in this moment, and that we are equipped to benefit and learn from what arises. In this mental state, we can accept another person and provide an open heart that allows us to share in the fullness of the other person's experience. Vulnerability welcomes another person's experience and thus powerfully encourages a connection to arise. If a connection doesn't arise when we are in this place, it is probably because the other person fears such a connection and is erecting some defense. When that happens—when someone resists our vulnerability—we may feel pain from the other person's unwillingness to accept the gift of our openness. But we can remain present, and simply accept that this moment is not the right one for the other person to connect, for whatever reason.

It seems paradoxical that vulnerability is not weakness—it is incredibly powerful. It is almost irresistibly attractive and tends to bring out the best in those around us. Thus, vulnerability is a powerful tool with which to influence people. If we attempt to use our vulnerability to manipulate others, it is not true vulnerability, since vulnerability is always genuine. If you're vulnerable, you see that what's best for the other person is what's best for you—you do not, you will not, act in manipulative ways. True connection is always mutually positive.

Imagine you and I have a big argument that hurt both of our feelings. The argument began because I thought you had done something to hurt me. I believe that you intended me some harm, or that you acted unfairly. You believe that I was the one who acted unfairly. How can we overcome this impasse?

If we can each achieve a state of vulnerability where we let down our defenses, we will each release the need to be right.

We will see that it does not matter who was right or wrong. In fact, the very concepts of right and wrong will cease to have any meaning. What happens instead is that we'll both begin to feel a comfort and a warmth of connection: a belonging in the moment. A trust will naturally arise out of that connection. We each feel safe saying, "I don't want to hurt you, I am sorry." This apology allows both of us to release the negativity and judgment that was blocking the flow of our connection. In the place once occupied by negativity, love will arise and deepen the connection. We can see that concepts such as "fault" or "right and wrong" are irrelevant. What matters is our connection, which starts with vulnerability.

Once again, it is paradoxical that the one who first apologizes, the one who first risks vulnerability, is actually the one who is first empowered. Vulnerability, therefore, is simultaneously gentle and extremely powerful. The one most vulnerable is the one who most powerfully harnesses the power of love.

This scenario is possible between almost any two people. As I said at the beginning of the book, I believe leading with love is always the right answer. That's not only true in romantic and familial relationships, but in politics, business—in all relationships. And it can happen fast, even with someone you've just met. Unfortunately, most people are not aware of this and act as though strength requires mental distance, defensiveness, or for them to come at others "playing offense." This happens because most people are controlled by their ego. The ego, by its very essence, understands only a life of division, separation, and competition. The ego believes that for you to win, I must lose. It subscribes to the belief that life is a zero-sum game, whereby one person's victory is another person's defeat. This is an unfortunate and costly error. It is completely incorrect.

Modern American politics is a great example of the belief in the zero-sum game. Politicians of the two major parties spend their time tearing the other side down, insulting them, or trying to defeat them. They have no interest in helping the other party, believing that any harm to their perceived opponent strengthens them. If the other party wins, they consider it a loss to themselves and their party. Conversely, in order to win, they feel the other party must lose. There's little collaboration for the greater good of the country, since neither party is operating in accordance with the truth: that what is good for one party is actually what is good for both parties. That is, making the country a better place for all of us means we all win. That which helps one, usually helps all.

If someone from either party could become truly vulnerable, and in that state of vulnerability understand that what is best for Democrat Chuck Schumer's grandchildren is also what is best for Republican Mitch McConnell's grandchildren, they could come to a place of understanding and connection. That would lead to agreements, progress for the greater good, for each party.

Would that be easy? No. But it is possible if each person learned to be vulnerable. What makes such healthy interaction so rare in politics is that most people, and perhaps especially most politicians, are operating from a mental state dominated by ego. As such, they operate from a paranoid, defensive, and fear-based point of view that prevents vulnerability and connection. This point of view tends to trigger a similar defensive reaction from others, thereby further inhibiting any real connection or cooperation.

When we are in a state of vulnerability, that state invites others to become vulnerable. They drop their defenses, and are more open to a connection. They correctly surmise that, being in a vulnerable state, we won't attack them. Trust develops. There is a feeling of safety, and in that safety, each of us feels at liberty to be fully ourselves. Each of us has an increased capacity to connect. The ensuing connection allows each of us to better experience truth, which is the strength, clarity, and power of love.

There's no effort in vulnerability. You're not trying to be seen as something you're not. It may not be easy because you're allowing yourself to be exposed in front of somebody. You are communicating, "Here I am complete with my imperfections and limitations, trusting you." When you bring that energy into a room, other people tend to gravitate toward it.

If someone is around you while you are in a state of vulnerability, your vulnerability will cause some feelings to stir in them. They may initially feel uncomfortable, which they may express as nervous chatter. If you can accept their nervousness and their chatter for a minute, and just nod and smile, they might come to a point where they start to realize they are chattering. Allow that moment. That vulnerability you hold continues to invite them into a more genuine connection. They may then relax some of their drama and become more present. Bringing vulnerability into a situation tends to defuse drama. Like eliminating oxygen diminishes a flame, removing oxygen from someone's drama (by being present and vulnerable) diminishes the drama. It begins to fizzle out, leaving a quiet space where there is room for a deep connection to form. That won't always happen, but it is effective often enough to make it an excellent strategy. If the other person is threatened by the vulnerability, they might not accept your invitation. But that is OK. Their time may come later.

When we make ourselves vulnerable, we participate in something sacred. That's not to say we won't regress into unhealthy behaviors or that our egos won't sometimes get the better of us. The human condition is ever changing, and it is natural to regress and backtrack into places of less spiritual wakefulness. But if one person brings vulnerability and presence to a situation, that act is a powerful invitation to others. Even if others don't realize it consciously, they will subconsciously be aware of the openness around them, and they'll want to pour themselves into that openness. They'll want to unite with the undeniable attractiveness and power of truth, love, and God. This reminds me of the saying in the field of physics, that "nature abhors a vacuum." It is a helpful principle to remember because when we create mental openness, emptiness, or space, that which comes rushing in to fill it is that which is all around us: love.

We can see how this desire to join others in their vulnerability happens when we attend a concert, where the artist sings a beautiful, touching song. People in the audience will soften, begin to sing, perhaps even cry, and embrace the people around them, even if they are strangers. Likewise, if one person approaches the other, and instead of reaching out a hand for a handshake, opens their arms inviting an embrace, the other person will almost never deny them. I know this because I personally often ignore an outstretched hand, and instead offer a hug. People almost always reciprocate. For this reason, leading with vulnerability and warmth is usually a great strategy to invite deeper connection, warmth, camaraderie, and cooperation. Who wouldn't want a life with more of these awesome qualities?

VULNERABILITY WORKS EVERYWHERE

I've worked with thousands of men and women, many of them in positions that reported to me, especially during my twenty years as a CEO. When I communicated with people, they would often place me in a position of prominence due to my fancy title. "Oh my gosh," they would say. "I cannot believe that I am meeting with the CEO!"

I always did my best to deflate this artificial point of differentiation between us. I reminded them that I was just another person, no more special or elite than they were. That I was a person with real world struggles, joys, and silliness. As part of this, I often shared something personal about my life that might affect my work. I might say, "Oh, I was up all night with my kids, and I'm kind of tired today." Doing this exposed me. It demonstrated my vulnerability. This, in turn, let them know it was OK to tell me about themselves. I never pushed anyone to disclose anything about their personal life. But I made it feel very normal to do so, so they often ended up sharing a lot. I was always looking for opportunities to connect with people.

If I saw someone holding back, I might say to them, "I notice you tend to be quieter during meetings. I want to make sure I don't bowl you over, because I can be pretty intense."

They might laugh and say, "Well, a little intense, but I'm getting used to it."

That's an opportunity to go deeper. "If you say you're 'getting used to it,' that means I've probably shut you down a little bit. I'm really sorry, I don't want to do that. I want to have a relationship where you feel at liberty to tell me what's on your mind. Tell me more!"

This is leading with vulnerability.

People are hesitant to be vulnerable because it initially feels weak. When we feel vulnerable, we feel our limitations. We can feel it physically—it tickles. Our heart feels exposed, and a bit raw. We feel susceptible to the outside forces of the world. And indeed, we are! To be vulnerable entails a leap of faith. It means trusting the world around you. It's like laying yourself in the hands of God. You have to believe that the hands of God will not steer you wrong or harm you. However, once you are able to be vulnerable, then you tap into the source of all power, all glory, all wisdom, all knowledge that exists in the universe. You become a conduit for it. This is true because the truth that is love that is God exists all around us at every moment, and when we are open-hearted, vulnerable, and present, we can feel it. We can tap into it. We can let this power and natural intelligence flow through us.

We will find that more power comes to us when we allow ourselves to be a conduit not only for our own learned intelligence, but also for the vast intelligence that exists all around us. If we develop a keen awareness, we can tap into this vast sea of intelligence and knowledge. This entails surrender. We need to become aware of the vastness that exists in the world outside and allow our curiosity and perceptivity to develop as much as possible. If we do this, we find we are quite powerful.

There are other examples of where vulnerability, perhaps counterintuitively, leads us to be in a powerful position. For instance, when a person confronts violence with peace and vulnerability (as Dr. Martin Luther King taught during his years of non-violent protest) and even accepts being physically struck by an aggressor without fighting back, they effectively disempower the aggressor by showing them to be an unsympathetic bully, and even a coward.

THE POWER OF CURIOSITY

Curiosity is a desire to know and understand more about others and the world around us, and is critical to our journey to enjoy deeper and more meaningful relationships. Curiosity leads us to ask questions, and many of my deepest connections have arisen in the aftermath of such questions.

Questions that come from a desire to learn are almost always welcomed by the person being asked, even if they are relatively personal or probing, since the other person feels they've become our teacher, and thereby feels valued and empowered. On the contrary, questions that come not from curiosity, but from a place of judgment or manipulation, are seldom welcome as they put the person who's being asked in a defensive and disempowered position. Put differently, you cannot be curious and judgmental at the same time. The two concepts repel each other, and this has important implications.

When you ask someone a question because you really want to know them, or learn from them, you are essentially promoting them to being, at least for that moment, your teacher. Being a teacher is an honor: a position of distinction. By asking a question, one is subordinating oneself to another. Showing a kind of reverence for them. For this reason, questions can be very empowering to the person to whom they are asked. People feel honored and respected when you ask them questions in this way.

My wife recently told me she hates when people ask her questions. That surprised me, and I was curious why this was so. When I inquired more deeply why questions bothered her (by asking questions...hah!) I quickly found out that it was not the questions that bothered her. It was the judgment inherent in many of the questions. For instance, if she'd had a relatively quiet day, she may not like the question, "what have you been up to today?" because she does not want to feel the defensive feeling of being judged for not "doing" much. It is not questions, but her fear of the judgment inherent in certain questions that she doesn't like. I saw some proof of this when my questions to her about why questions bothered her didn't bother her at all. This was because my questions were asked not to judge, but to better understand her. Again, people love to be understood.

I can completely relate to her feelings. I remember when I was a child, my mother would sometimes ask me "what do you plan on doing with your summer?" I hated this question! I knew what she was really saying was that she wanted me to get busy with something, so I wouldn't "sit around all summer." She wasn't really curious at all! She knew darn well I had no plans. I hated how such questions triggered a feeling in me that what I was up to was not good enough. That somehow if I didn't do enough I'd be judged negatively. These are examples of where questions come not from curiosity, but instead from either a negative judgment or a place of manipulation.

I have always been very curious. More times than I can count, I've asked the questions which others were afraid to ask. I remember as a young boy asking my mom and dad loads of questions. I wanted to know everything they knew. While my mom was more patient with me, my constant questions drove my dad nuts. I had to learn to ask him questions in a way that would make him more likely to answer. This technique involved reading his mood and learning to ask questions with a great deal of respect, even reverence. When I got this right, he usually gave me a good answer. I think this skill, developed to harness my dad's treasure trove of knowledge, gave me a head start asking questions of others.

Curiosity is a natural state for any animal, and certainly for human beings. In a world where we know almost nothing of the vastness which surrounds us, how could we be awake without also being intensely curious? Think about young kids—curiosity is their natural approach to the world. But this tends to diminish as we become adults. We become afraid, we withdraw and become more careful. It needn't be this way. We benefit from cultivating and encouraging our own curiosity, which is inherently positive, incredibly powerful, and the birthplace of almost all understanding.

Beginning relationships with curiosity is powerful, because

again, when we're curious, we are not judgmental. Therefore, when we begin with curiosity, we invite others to pour themselves into our curiosity. They feel safe doing so, since we are providing a safe space for them, free of judgment. In that space, people feel safe and trusting. This leads them to become vulnerable.

Unfortunately, people tend to believe that the best way to get to know another person is to ask about the other person's story. There's a related belief that people are, essentially, the sum total of their life experiences. But this is not the case. People are not limited by their life story any more than a flash drive is limited by the music that someone records on it. This is important, because so often these days, when getting to know each other, people's first questions are potentially offensive, and often limiting. For instance, the question, "So what do you do?" is potentially offensive, since the person asking appears ready to judge you based on your answer. If you answer, "I'm homeless and unemployed," the person asking you will likely feel differently about you than if you answer, "I am a neurosurgeon." The former answer is deemed to accompany someone less deserving of respect and admiration, and the second answer is deemed to accompany someone more deserving of attention and admiration. But such a conclusion does not allow the person negatively judged to be seen and valued, as they deserve to be. In fact, even the person being positively judged may be disadvantaged by the resulting judgment.

An example of this occurred when I was working as the co-CEO of Chipotle. Often, when someone asked me, "So, what do you do?" I would answer "Oh, I work for Chipotle!" Often, that answer led me to have positive conversations with people, since at that time Chipotle seemed almost universally loved. My kids often asked me, "Dad, why didn't you tell them that you were the CEO?" When they asked this, I would explain that sometimes by telling someone I was CEO, I would essentially hijack the whole conversation. It would bring an undue amount of attention to me and my career, often inhibiting my ability to get to know the other person as quickly or deeply.

Understanding that "who someone is" not the same as "their story" is of critical importance in connecting to others. If you test this claim by avoiding asking someone about their story, you will be amazed at how much more quickly you can connect with people, and develop more interesting, trusting, and enduring relationships. For me, this came easily, since I am just much less interested in someone's story than I am interested in who they are. I am eager to make a connection with people who I meet, and throughout my life, I have found that people's stories don't do much to advance that connection. Instead, I really want to know who a person is: to feel a camaraderie with them, to feel the warmth of their heart.

Once I find a connection with them, then I might want to hear aspects of their story to better learn and understand how they came to be the way they are. But I've no positive or negative association, for instance, about their status or title or level of achievement. I'm just interested in the person in the room with me. Who is this being? This deep curiosity for who they are is often felt by those I meet as welcoming and warm, and people tend to respond very positively. It doesn't matter if it's the president of the United States, the Dalai Lama, or a homeless person in a café. Bringing curiosity and vulnerability is consistently welcomed. It leads to positive, exciting relationships. It leads to deep connections.

Once a connection begins to build, I tend to quickly dig deeper in order to better understand someone. If I sense something is off with someone I'm with, I'll typically ask, with real concern, "Is something the matter?" Usually, people will quickly let me know, and this deepens our connection. Other times, someone may be resistant to share what's going on. In such cases, I might ask again, "What's wrong?" I might ask a few times. I might say, "I'm only asking because I can tell something's not right." Normally, the person will then share with me what's on their mind.

I do this even with people I've met for the first time. If I sense something is off, I will ask, "Are you okay?" I'll ask it in a way that is curious and caring. People can tell because of my tone, posture, facial expression, and open-heartedness, that I truly care. You'd be surprised how most people, when they hear that question coming from a truly open-hearted, deeply curious and loving place, badly want an audience for what's going on with themselves. They want to be seen, valued, understood, and loved.

Everyone out there in the world is yearning for this sort of connection. Everyone. Some people are harder nuts to crack, but they're still yearning for it. Perhaps they have been hurt in the past, which leads them to fear becoming vulnerable. The fear of further pain causes defensiveness. When this occurs, it is most effective to give them the space and privacy they seem to favor, and just make them aware that you are there if they need you. Soon enough, many will come back, seeking some time with you.

I may be more insistent on finding connection than most because years of experience have shown me the value of it. I am quick to see beyond any initial defenses that might suggest someone else isn't as open to such a connection, because I know deep in my heart that they crave it. This habit has been the source of many wonderful and important connections throughout my life. Even though it can be painful to live in a state of constant sensitivity to the feelings of others around me, I wouldn't trade it. It has been a true gift in my life. It will be a gift to anyone who cultivates it.

When I met the Dalai Lama, who is very present, he asked nothing about what I did. Likewise, I asked him nothing about what he did. I was struck by how easy and satisfying it was to just be with him. We both chose to be present and we allowed love to flow through us. There was a feeling of openness, acceptance, comfort, vulnerability, familiarity, and love in the air. I didn't presume I needed to prove myself in order to justify his attention. We were just two people sharing a precious moment and a genuine and sacred connection. There was a lot of lightness and a lot of laughter. It felt magical.

I try to bring this same focus and attention to every person I meet. I fail at it sometimes. Sometimes I am "in the middle of something," self-absorbed and less available. But I try to bring presence and vulnerability even if it's only for a moment before we do whatever business there is to do between us. That second or two of presence will make the interaction special. In other words, when you bring presence to an interaction with someone, they will sense something is special, different, and sacred about your time together, no matter how short. This realization alone is enough motivation to convince me of the value of bringing curiosity, and the resulting presence, to every meeting.

PART II

Things that Interfere with the Flow of Love

As I discussed at length in Part I, love is everywhere: a universal force that is available to everyone as long as they allow it to flow into their lives. The reason human connections are so valuable is that they are the gateway to having love relationships with others. But how can we best connect? What is fascinating and exciting to me is that connections between people will arise naturally, without any effort, as long as nothing interferes. The trouble is, interference is more the norm than the exception. The primary forces that tend to interfere with our ability to connect with others are what I discuss in this Part II. If we learn to better understand these forces, we will dramatically improve our ability to connect with others, and therefore live life with more warmth, love, and understanding. These forces are the ego, defensiveness dysfunction, biases caused by the way we see things (which I call lenses), assumptions, the way we label the people and the world around us, and our own fear of discomfort.

CHAPTER 4

The Ego

Everyone has heard the term ego, but since there are many ways of defining or describing it, I will first explain what I mean when I use this term. I have found this understanding of the subject of ego to be extremely useful on my own journey of spiritual development.

WHAT IS THE EGO?

The ego is a psychological mechanism within all of us that begins to develop during the first several months of our lives as we begin to identify as being a separate person. The newborn infant initially has no sense of being a separate person. There is initially no awareness of "self" and "other." Think about it. Why would there be? You've just come out of your mother's womb, where you were linked to her heart, her body, her lungs, her life. You were literally a part of her moments ago. Why would it occur to you only seconds later, after a tiny journey down the birth canal, that suddenly you are separate? Psychologically, this sense of being an independent and separate "self" continues to develop during the first few years of our life.

By a few years of age, we have developed a sense of being a separate and distinct person, which sense is largely composed of our memories and our thoughts about what makes us unique and different in the world. This sense of self is the ego.

The ego develops as an inner voice in our head, or an assembly of qualities that we believe defines us as an individual to the rest of the world. It is our story. It's the sum total of all the labels by which we define our "self." Once we develop this ego, we tend to believe that it is us. That it is who we are. But it is NOT who we are, any more than a flash drive becomes the music that someone records onto it. The flash drive is NOT the music. Rather, the music is on the flash drive. The flash drive exists no matter what is recorded on it. It contains, but does not become, that which is recorded on it. Likewise, we humans develop a personality during our lives, and we develop certain habits, thoughts, ways of thinking, a sense of humor, and so forth. Those things are not "who we are," yet we often have difficulty differentiating ourselves from these characteristics we develop. Most people have difficulty understanding that they exist as a being which is totally independent of their personality, or story, or ego.

As we assemble an ever-increasing collection of thoughts about who we are, we start to think of ourselves as being those thoughts. This development of ego comes part and parcel with judgments about ourselves and others. Our egoic thinking believes certain of our characteristics are good, and others bad. We seek to have more good characteristics, and fewer bad ones. We also judge other people's characteristics as good or bad, and we constantly compare ourselves to others, feeling either superior or inferior. These judgments are often experienced as a voice in our head. Our ego is the "me" part of the voice in our head which asks, "What's in this for me? How does this help me? Is he here to help me, or harm me? How can I get more for me?"

HOW THE EGO DEVELOPS

When we're born, we're born present in the moment. Since the most important act for the preservation of any species is that its offspring survive to the age of reproduction, we human beings are wired to survive. We're born awake. We're born vulnerable. In some ways we're born in a spiritually enlightened state because we are born without having to carry the mantle of human existence yet, and without having to try to return to a place of presence. We are already quite present.

However, we're also born unable to survive without external support. As infants determined to survive, we quickly realize there are discomforts in the world. We get hungry, and we don't like that feeling. We get cold, and we don't like that feeling. Instinctively, we know that if we don't eat, we will die. If we don't drink, we will die. If we get too cold, we will die. If we get too warm, we will die. All of the instinct and brilliance of our nervous system is built to help us survive. Surviving means doing whatever is necessary to make sure our parents feed us, give us enough to drink, and keep us from getting too warm or too cold. We do what's necessary and the ego very quickly learns what works.

We cry when we're hungry in order to attract food. We cry when we're cold to attract a blanket. As we get older, we continue to sense what is going on around us, and in particular, the vibes that our parents are giving off. After all, evolution has favored those children who were very attuned to their parents because those were the children who survived. Today, if our parents are stressed out and worried about keeping a roof over our heads, if they're fighting and arguing a lot, we are threatened because anything that makes them unstable literally feels like it threatens our survival. It feels to us like not having food or water. We feel something is threatening our parents, and what threatens them, threatens us. If they have a lot of anxiety in their lives, we feel that anxiety as a threat. We start to come up with techniques to ameliorate those negative vibrations from our parents. We become very good at this, because children are incredibly present and observant, and our parents are, roughly speaking, our entire universe. We take on the task of comforting them so they will be able to take care of us.

As we get older, the behaviors we found most effective as an infant and child become habitual. They begin to form what we call our personality and our egoic structure. In my case, I got the sense I wasn't wanted by my father. I learned to do things to make him come toward me, to want me more. This was hard work! I sought his acceptance and his warmth. I became very conscious of how my presence disturbed him—walking too loudly, making too much noise—so I got good at not pissing him off. I learned to walk on eggshells.

I got good not just at accommodating my father but accommodating nearly everyone I encountered. Like so many habitual behaviors, this had both positive and negative impacts on my life. Because I am so sensitive to others, so accommodating, I have highly honed my ability to figure out what pleases people. I am keenly aware through another person's body language, for instance, whether an interaction is going well or not, and I can adjust in milliseconds. I have earned a lot of worldly success because of this. I draw a lot of positive attention. I get raises and promotions. I am offered big jobs. I succeed at those jobs and receive many material rewards. My ego likes this. But there is a significant cost.

It has been very difficult to extricate myself from my own egoic structure. I have found that I am so accommodating that

I tend to sacrifice my own needs for someone else's affection or positive attention. If someone else comes into a room and is having a bad day, I find it very difficult not to focus all my attention on working to eradicate their pain, anger, or frustration. At times, I give myself away and am not true to myself. I sometimes don't concern myself enough that my own needs are not being met. In fact, I am often so keen to please others that I may not even know what my needs are. I am habitually in a place where I first seek to secure the comfort of those around me, which means I'm often not able to operate as a fully independent person. If I do this too much, it can cause me to feel frustrated and resentful.

This is residue from the habitual survival behaviors I developed as a child and that my ego still values. Getting out of this mindset requires becoming aware of my behavior. It requires bringing presence into those moments and noticing how I get caught up in my habits. I can become aware, and when I am aware I can choose not to follow the patterns I developed when I was eight or ten or twelve years old. I can choose not to play that same old record again. But it is a challenge because old habits die hard.

THE EGO AT WORK

Coming to understand this tricky and highly camouflaged mechanism within us is very difficult at first. I find that one of the best ways to understand when we're experiencing our ego is to learn some of its telltale signs.

The first sign is a dissatisfaction with the present moment. The ego is always keenly concerned about finding future pleasure or avoiding future pain. The ego is afraid and permanently insecure. It is not ever satisfied with things as they are in the present moment, except for during brief moments after a major "victory." Generally, the ego views the present moment as only having value insofar as it will carry us to a better future. The ego's constant insecurity makes great sense: if your only salvation lies in the future, and the future by definition is uncertain, that is a recipe for insecurity. The ego is always rejecting what is and wanting something different, something more. This means it can never rest. It can never be satisfied. It is also competitive, always seeking to prove itself right or others wrong.

In my life I've had a lot of ego "wins"—achieving material success and public recognition. I know what that feels like. When I think of my ego in those moments of achievement, I think of the famous image of Tiger Woods pumping his fist after sinking his last putt to win the Masters. That's what the ego looks like in action. It's saying, "Yes! I've done it! I've succeeded!" As I've mentioned, such moments are incredibly fleeting.

In my experience, when you begin to become aware of the egoic self that you've created during your lifetime, you will begin to awaken. You cannot turn back. When you realize that you are not your ego, it will become harder to be satisfied again with pursuing purely egoic victories. The reason for this is you quickly become aware that the egoic victories are not lastingly satisfying. They are illusory, fleeting, and impermanent. They are based on a false understanding of what matters.

For instance, we see wealthy people in the media every day who cannot stop the pursuit of money. They have a nice house and lots of dough in the bank. Yet their ego is not satisfied. Their ego says, "I've only got X dollars. Jeff Bezos and Elon Musk have hundreds or thousands of times that! I've got to get more money! Look at my house—it's nothing compared to the houses on the golf course in Pebble Beach. Those houses are way nicer! Those people must be much happier! And yeah, I'm healthy, but I can't ride a bike as fast as that guy. He's got a better physique. I need to be in better shape!"

Everyone wants to be seen, valued, understood, and loved, but most people go about it the wrong way. Most go out into the world and try to become rich and famous. They try to become powerful. They do this because they want to feel valuable. They think that material achievements might cause other people to value them more. But these material achievements don't cause you to be loved or valued or understood or cared for. In fact, those things probably have the *opposite* effect, because the more powerful, rich, and famous you become, the less other people will think you need to be seen, valued, understood, and loved. They will assume that since you have it all, you don't need them, or value them. This tends to create distance, and to impede connection.

Wealth, fame, and power, therefore, tend to act as impediments to other people seeing you, valuing you, understanding you, loving you. Other people might want your autograph, but that doesn't mean they know who you are. If you're Kevin Hart or Roger Federer, people don't necessarily want to shake your hand because they value *you*. They want to shake your hand because they value your comedic talent or your tennis prowess. They think meeting you will make them feel more valuable to their friends. None of this has to do with actually valuing you as a person.

If you're any kind of star, people value your accomplishment. That's what they're attracted to. But accomplishments are fleeting. They don't exist once they're over. Instead, everyone looks for your next accomplishment. Over time, as a tennis star, for instance, you'll be able to accomplish less and less. The crowds and the television cameras will go away. What will be left? Often, what's left for "stars" is a feeling of emptiness. A feeling of loss. This is why famous people so often struggle with depression when the spotlight on their career dims. They often resort to substance abuse or other self-destructive behaviors to try to preserve the egoic high that their fame allowed them to experience. On and on it goes. The ego is never satisfied. The ego never has enough. The ego never arrives.

The ego thinks the world is a zero-sum game and that another person's victory is our defeat: that their win is our loss. It sees others only as a means to an end. The ego cannot love others, although it freely uses the word love, and even tricks us into thinking we feel love when it identifies someone that it thinks will give it more of what it wants, craves, and needs. While the ego cannot love others, it will certainly use others!

The ego is always using terms like "better" and "worse," making judgments and comparisons. It values things like status, success, money, fame, prestige, accomplishments. But the ego is tricky. It is also the part of you that says you are weak, deficient, unworthy, no good, a failure, and so forth. (Even when you win a gold medal, right after that victory, it immediately sets about thinking, "Now what?")

We know our ego is operating anytime we are:

- Judging something as good or bad.
- Comparing ourselves to others.
- Trying to prove ourselves right or prove another person wrong.
- Rejecting the present moment in favor of a better future.
- Obsessing about our past.
- Hearing a voice in our head.
- Feeling dissatisfied with who we are.

- Wanting credit for something.
- Wanting to have power over others.
- Wanting to be better than others.
- Wanting anything to be other than how it is.
- Feeling rejection or dissatisfaction.

But if you are curious, that is not ego. If you are focused on the task at hand with all of your attention, that is not ego. If you are aware and watching to see what will happen next, with anticipation, that is not ego. If you are 100 percent engaged in anything at this very moment, with all of your concentration, that is not ego, because you are living in the present moment.

Do not confuse ego with achieving something excellent. Or mastering a skill. Or working hard to learn more. It is our natural human state to grow, blossom, develop, learn, and deepen our spiritual connection to the truth, to love, and to God. When we are curious and want to understand more, when we seek the truth and want to better understand our world, that is not ego.

The ego is perhaps the trickiest challenge we have in understanding the truth about ourselves, each other, and the universe we live in.

If we are operating from our ego, that means that we are dissatisfied with the present moment. It means that we are struggling to build ourselves up to be something more, since we are not satisfied with who we are now. In this state of mind, there is no room to bring openness and vulnerability to another person, because we are self-focused. Therefore, there is no love. No feeling of love for them, and no love for ourselves. After all, since love can only happen in reality (remember, truth, love, and God are the same thing), and the only reality is the present moment, and the ego cannot live in the present moment, then there is no love unless we can become present, open, and vulnerable to what exists in the here and now.

The problem is not that the ego is bad or that we shouldn't have an ego. The problem is that we confuse it with being who we are. It can become our whole self-image, and we're at risk of forgetting that there is anything else besides it. It renders us spiritually asleep, unaware, unable to be in touch with truth, love, and God. A full-blown identification with the ego prevents us from having a connection with that which is real and true.

The ego doesn't understand what enriches us. It is very skilled at misdirection. In the first chapter I described how we can make space and allow love to fill that space. The ego resists that. Space freaks the ego out! The ego can't stand space. So, the ego is very adept at filling space, eliminating space, sometimes in ways that may not look like the ego at all. For example, people who consciously seek enlightenment may find themselves filling space with reading about enlightenment, talking about enlightenment, acting like they're enlightened.

They join groups of people who support the notion that they are important, and more enlightened than others. If they are part of a group of people seeking enlightenment, they may fall into the same kind of competition we see in other distracting human pursuits that often put the ego front and center, like constantly seeking more wealth, or a bigger house or more expensive car. People will compete, subconsciously, to be the most enlightened—which of course demonstrates a complete lack of enlightenment, since it is their ego that is competing. If they do begin to awaken, they may become aware that they have built an enormous ego structure around the very process of becoming enlightened.

Importantly, the ego has no interest in your spiritual well-being, or love, fulfillment, or the present moment. In fact, it is usually bored by the present moment, because the present moment is exactly what the ego rejects in its ceaseless effort to obtain a better future. Since the present moment is the only place where we can live, can love, can truly be, the ego is neither interested in nor capable of feeling love! This inability of the ego to feel or experience the boundless and infinite power, joy, and glory of love is one of the major reasons that understanding the ego, and finding some space from it, is so worthwhile. If we do not find space from the ego, we are forever relegated to dissatisfaction, judgment, frustration, and delusion. Why delusion? Because anything besides the present moment is not real, and anything that is not real is delusion.

YOU ARE NOT YOUR PERSONALITY

Personality and ego are not exactly the same, but there's a great deal of similarity. We develop character traits—personality—that are not directly the ego, but they arise out of the ego. To understand this concept, think about oysters. Every oyster shell is unique, even though oyster shells have similarities that allow us to see them as oysters. Every oyster shell looks different because the oyster created it in response to its environment. The personality works the same way. We construct our personality, including our character traits, in response to the environment.

You might say, "I never lie." That's a character trait. It's also almost certainly a product of your ego believing that honesty is a required element of believing "I am good." The oyster shell isn't the living creature. The personality is not the living person or true self. The true self lies beneath the personality. The true self is that which is aware that there is an ego at work. The true self can observe the ego.

The ego standing in for the self gets in the way of connection because the ego doesn't know how to look at someone else except as someone to use. The ego wants to use others to derive benefit from them, like money or status, or to allow us to feel better about ourselves by comparing ourselves favorably to another person. The ego thrives on comparison. It is always trying to be better, richer, stronger, prettier, smarter. If you are stuck in your ego, you will not truly care for others. You will see them only insofar as they can help you add to your pile of accomplishments. Since most people don't know that they exist beyond the ego, they don't know where the ego stops and how to develop relationships with other people that are genuine and not manipulative. This book is not about freeing yourself from your ego—there are many books about that, not to mention whole spiritual practices such as Buddhism—but it is important to understand that you are not going to have deep connections with people if you are only operating from ego.

To prevent dysfunction that gets in the way of connection, we must become aware of the ego and observe it in action.

There is only one effective method I know of that seems to really help make sure that we do not make decisions solely to satisfy our ego, and that is to notice our ego at work. Be a witness to it. Watch it. Know when it is there, and just be aware of it. By doing so, it begins to soften, and release its grip on us, such that we can make decisions from a place of strength and awareness, not fear and reactivity.

IF WE'RE NOT EGO, WHAT ARE WE?

It is very important to understand that our ego is not who we are. But if that is true, then who are we beyond ego?

The truth is that we are an outgrowth of the essential nature of God. We are an outgrowth, a manifestation, of the substrate that is the very truth we seek to understand. We are not separate from truth, or from God. So, we are free to partake of God, know God, understand God, and to the best of our limited human capacities, live as one with God. By opening up to our interconnectedness with all that is true, good, and real, we can partake of and enjoy an awareness, intelligence, and understanding that is far greater than our limited faculties would otherwise allow.

This, I believe, is the meaning of life. To increasingly open ourselves to the discovery and understanding of the truth, such that we can live the fullest, richest, and deepest life experience we can, and to the extent possible, become one with the truth.

We all exist as a living embodiment of the very consciousness that is ubiquitous throughout the universe. We are, essentially, an outgrowth of truth, love, and God. The Christians say that we are children of God, and hence often begin prayers with the words "Our father." Even if you are not Christian, you can easily accept that there is some force, entity, being, intelligence, or consciousness from which you came. Even if you believe you are the manifestation of an incredibly complex science experiment, then it is clearly a pretty amazing, unbelievably complex science experiment!

You are a creation of that. You are the offspring of brilliance and vast intelligence. You are an outgrowth of that which gave birth to the whole universe. You exist as a living embodiment of that great force. You emanate from, and remain part of, an incredibly complex entity, being and wisdom that is brilliantly balanced, unimaginably intelligent, infinitely wise, and cease-lessly giving. You come, in essence, from that which is most great and most good. You are a conscious, living, aware being. And that being that you are I will call your "true self."

This nomenclature is obviously faulty, since even the word "self" contemplates something that you are not, which is a sep-arate being. You are not separate. You have your own name, your own clothing, and your own shoes, but your true self is not really a separate being. Instead, you are a living embodiment of the universal consciousness. You came from the universe, and you are living this life, and then you will continue to be part of the universe. When you really think about it this way, you can get a healthier outlook on your life. You begin to realize that you are on the one hand not that big a deal, which is kind of a relief, and that you are also a sacred piece of God, which is sort of cool.

Your true self does not depend on anything. It can't be hurt by criticism and doesn't depend on another's approval. It exists independently of your ego. It is the part of you that can love others (in fact, your essential nature is love, and therefore your true self cannot NOT love others!). In fact, your essen-tial nature really isn't *a part of* you at all. Rather, your essential nature IS your true self. This essential nature is awareness, is presence, is love, is God, is authenticity. It is really NOT most accurate to say that your essential nature is even yours at all. The reason for this is that this "true self" is not separate from truth, love, or God, but rather is part of truth, love, and God.

Does that mean I am saying that our true selves are God? No. What I am saying is that our true self is not separate from God, just as a tree is not separate from Earth. Is a tree Earth? No. But is a tree separate from Earth? No. It is not separate from Earth. Is a tree an offshoot of Earth? Part of Earth? A piece of Earth? Yes. It is.

Likewise, you are an offshoot of God, a piece of God, part of God. When you are able to create a little space between you and your ego, relinquish judgment, become aware, become one with the present moment, one with truth, and love, then yes, you are an offshoot of God. A piece of God. You are, at that moment, one with God. It is not accurate to say that you are God, because that would limit God to the confines of your experience. And God is not limited. We as humans tend to limit ourselves, but we needn't limit our experience to what we experience physically, nor to what we experience mentally. We can open ourselves to a broader experience. We are not God. But we can, by allowing a deep connection with truth, love, and God, participate and partake in the love that flows from God, which means we can experience a vast beauty, intelligence, awareness, and magic that would otherwise be well beyond our abilities, by allowing that connection. This is the magic of life. That we are invited to have a sacred connection with truth. With love. With God.

THE EGO IS ALWAYS WITH US

You can always tell when the source of a pleasant psychological sensation is derived from the ego. It sounds like, "Fuck yeah!" Or, "Damn, I'm good!" It contains a feeling of pride. Of having summited a great peak. It is about beating others. It's about winning. It's about you. "I'm good. I've made it. I've succeeded. Finally!" It is a feeling that's temporary. It doesn't belong to everyone.

But when one feels the warmth of the real satisfaction that comes from connection, instead of "Damn, I'm good," they might think, "This is good." Instead of, "I'm winning," it's "This is good." Instead of thinking, "I've summited this peak," it's "What a spectacular summit." Instead of being a personal victory, it's the realization that the stuff of the universe, the foundation of everything, is a complete unifying love that is free. Infinite. Abundant. It feels like a celebration that is inclusive, cooperative, and unifying.

It's our egoic human nature to try to harness it. Store it. Keep it. Hoard it. Claim it. Make it permanent. Marry it. Name it. Stay with it. Show it off. Write about it. Make it our own. The human mind, dominated by ego, often is unaware of any other way to react in the face of this enormous and very humbling glorious reality of infinite love.

Really, rather than containing, solidifying, or possessing something, love is about sharing the abundance we've found.

It's about watching greatness as an appreciative audience. Swimming in a warm and infinite ocean and just marveling in gratitude. Finding a gold nugget in the river, admiring its beauty and how it feels in our hands, understanding its value, then setting it back in the river.

But we humans want to keep greatness once we find it. Of course we do! Why do you think there's always a bunch of real estate offices in some of the world's most beautiful places? We want to preserve this moment forever. Buy a house. Preserve the magic we feel now. But then we find that which we are trying to preserve is not a place, but a state of mind. A momentary fleeting sensation that we'd love to make permanent. We'd rather make something that feels good permanent than trust that more greatness is available if we allow this moment and the next to be whatever arises.

Moments aren't forever. They're about fluidity. They're about timelessness. They're inherently temporary. It's their temporary nature that makes them rare and precious and price-less and irreplaceable. Allowing, accepting, and trusting this moment is the path to connection. And until we can manage that, it's ok. We'll do the best we can.

If the ego seems "bad" after my definition, I understand. In fact, millions of spiritual seekers for thousands of years have sought to eradicate the ego to achieve enlightenment. But what is funny is that when we hear a voice in our head that says "Shit, I want to get rid of that ego he's talking about," that IS our ego talking! If we hear a voice saying "Oh, well, I don't really have an ego," that IS our ego talking! If we hear a voice saying, "Well, at least my ego isn't as big as that guy's ego," that IS our ego talking!

Paradoxically, to avoid building our egos further, it's important not to seek to get rid of your ego. By seeking to get rid of it, you strengthen it, because the very "you" that is trying to get rid of it, is it! (That is why it is fair to say that the ego is very sneaky.) By becoming aggressive towards ourselves we merely strengthen our ego, since the aggression emanates from the ego.

The most effective tool to allow us to begin to gain some space and freedom from the grip of the ego is simply to become aware of it. Our awareness is not our ego. Awareness arises only by being in touch with and interested in what is arising in our immediate experience, and the ego has no interest in this. When we are aware, that awareness is our true self. The self that isn't dependent on anything. That self is indestructible. That self is unafraid. Strong. Genuine. Connected to the truth. Capable of loving.

Awareness implies presence. Being here, now. How do we know when we are here now? Well, in those moments there is no voice in our head. There is no judgment of good or bad. No desire to label things. No desire to take a photo. No effort to alter what is occurring. No desire to make it permanent, to marry it, to own it, to have it forever. Just appreciation, awareness, curiosity, attention. If you are like most people, you will notice that such moments are uncommon. But such moments are always available to all of us. Such moments are when we are truly alive.

When we are only operating from our ego, we are not present. We can't see anyone. We can't value anyone. We can't understand anyone. We can't love anyone. Because you can only do these things when there is a you to do it. And you are NOT your ego!

When we become aware of our ego, and get in touch with our essential nature, we can access our vulnerability, and become present, awake, and available for other people.

MANAGING THE EGO

Have you ever gone on a beach vacation? The first day on the beach is great. You feel so happy to be there. The waves, the sun, the sea birds, they're all fresh and wonderful. The second day is good, but it is less fresh and surprising. The third day you may start to wonder what to do with your time. In other words, constant vacation—which we often equate with happiness—will become routine. Once it is routine, you won't feel as excited. Likewise, happiness cannot exist as a permanent state of being. Joy can. Contentment can. Serenity can. But not happiness.

Of course, most people would prefer to feel happy than some other state—I certainly do! Those moments when I feel happy are really pleasant. They feel nice. But happiness is a product of a yin-yang experience. It is relative. Happiness depends on being able to experience feelings that are not happiness. If you were happy all the time, that would begin to feel normal. You wouldn't feel it as happiness because you'd experience a shifting baseline.

One immense gift we can give ourselves during our lives here on Earth is to stop trying to escape hardship and struggle, and rather accept what comes to us as the exact experience that is needed for our spiritual growth. By accepting it, I don't mean merely "putting up with it," but feeling gratitude for it. Only by feeling gratitude for it do you cease rejecting it, which means you can now open your heart, feel vulnerable, and allow love again to flow through you. Even in hardship and struggle, you can find love! It is a hell of a lot more pleasant to go through life's tougher moments with gratitude and love than it is to go through them with rejection and disgust. Also, the former means you won't suffer, and the latter means you will! Because feeling rejection and disgust are simply adding negativity and suffering to that which is already a challenge. This makes no sense.

If happiness itself—what the ego constantly pursues—isn't a laudable goal, what is?

Finding inner peace. A kind of warm and rich contentment, which arises from being totally present, aware, and in touch with the truth that is love and is God. That's a laudable goal. It comes when we set our ego aside for a few moments.

Achieving this, even briefly, can bring about a richer, more satisfying life experience than the version our culture tells us to pursue. If you can learn to accept what is, relax into the truth of the moment, allow what is simply to be, then you can watch as the ego rejects aspects of your experience. When that happens, you can practice letting go of the rejection, and returning to acceptance. A space free of thoughts and judgments then develops, and there's warmth and vast intelligence in that space. There's a feeling of being possessed of and supported by something that is vastly wise and strong and innately intelligent. It is supportive and comforting and enriching. This space allows us to become one with something profound and infinitely powerful. This something, which has been given many names (universal consciousness and God among them) is what I'm suggesting is simply love. We feel held in the embrace of a strength, calm, peace, and wisdom that we don't need to earn. It is love. Love is truth. Love is the endpoint. Finding and inhabiting this place is a much more laudable goal than chasing happiness.

But there is a problem with making it our goal to find this place: by making it our goal, we engage the ego. By "trying to get there" we begin to reject the reality that we are in right at this moment. Again, the mechanism in our lives that rejects the present moment is the ego, and the ego can't tolerate this place I am describing. The ego doesn't value it, since it can't be earned. Unity with love is not something someone arrives at when they deserve it, or when they've worked long and hard enough. Rather, it is something that happens when we can fully allow, forgive, accept, and bring gratitude to each moment in our lives as it arises. To allow what is, without judgment or clinging or trying to possess this magical space. That is tough to do, because when we experience this sacred place, which feels magical, our ego tends to rush in to possess it, own it, keep it, and call it an achievement. But it cannot be owned or possessed, since like air, it is not ours to own. But, wonderfully, it is completely unnecessary to own or possess it since it is infinite and omnipresent.

When we inhabit the space I'm describing, our perceptions rise to a very high level. We hear things we weren't hearing before, smell things we didn't smell, see things we didn't see, and experience a depth in each moment which allows us to experience its inherent brilliance. If everyone in the world inhabited this space more often, they'd have access to an innate intelligence that isn't learned, but simply understood. An intelligence that comes with our wiring. It allows us to tap into something much greater than ourselves, a connection with truth, which is love, which is God. Something exhilarating, brilliant, and fascinating, which at the same time is completely ordinary, peaceful and calm.

This, to me, is the most worthwhile thing that can happen to any of us during our time as human beings. But it is also the best thing that can happen to our species and our planet, since inhabiting this space means we understand the interconnectedness of all beings, and so we are loving and compassionate with one another. We will then be excellent stewards of our natural resources, and responsible leaders of our society.

CHAPTER 5

Assumptions

Tom and Nancy struggled mightily with their sixteen-year-old son Jason. For two years they were in a constant battle with him to stop smoking marijuana, which is legal in their state for adults. Jason struggled with friendships. He dropped out of school for a while. He hung out with a crowd of people who were not positive influences.

For a long time, Tom and Nancy escalated their confrontation with Jason. First, they told him he shouldn't use marijuana. They tried to convince him it was bad for him. When they found it, they took it away. They grounded him. They started drug-testing him. In turn, he started lying to them, going to greater and greater lengths to acquire and smoke marijuana—and succeeding. Their relationship erupted into open conflict with no prospect of getting better on the current path. Their son ran away numerous times, and when he turned seventeen, he got an apartment and wouldn't come back home. They threatened him, warned him, admonished him, but he refused to come home.

Tom and Nancy were losing the drug war with their son because they made a faulty assumption. They assumed that marijuana was the problem. It was not. Marijuana was a symptom of a deeper problem—a fear, a lack, an insecurity, or some other need within their son. He did not feel a connection that he longed to feel, and so did not feel safe, seen, valued, understood, or loved. He had a deep, unfulfilled longing. So long as his parents kept their focus on the symptom of marijuana, they failed to connect with their son, which only increased his longing and feeling of disconnected emptiness. What was necessary for them as parents was to understand and address their son's situation, and to help him to feel seen, valued, understood, and loved. Only by choosing to look past his drug use, by inquiring with compassion and vulnerability about him as a person, could they reconnect with the son they were losing. Doing that would not be easy, but it was necessary.

When they asked me for advice, I said that they should sit down with their son, tell him that they loved him, and that they were sorry that they had failed to understand what he was going through. To let him know how sorry they were that their relationship had deteriorated. To let him know that, starting immediately, they were going to respect his independence, and that they were no longer going to concern themselves with his marijuana use. No more criticism about it. No more drug testing. To explain that he was a free man and had their blessing to remain living on his own, as an adult. I also advised them to tell their son he was welcome at their home anytime, and that they would always be there for him.

While they both were surprised by what I said, and frightened to follow my advice, they did. They set their son free and committed to be there as a support for him if he wanted it. Over the next few months, Jason came by the house more and more. Their interactions became more positive. There was mutual respect. There was the feeling of love again between them. In time, Jason moved back into the family home.

When you make incorrect assumptions about someone, you can't really connect with them because you aren't really seeing them. You are only seeing what you are projecting onto them: your incorrect assumptions. That's what Tom and Nancy were doing. When they stopped doing this, things shifted. They regained their credibility as Jason's parents, he began to seek their advice and support once again, and a positive relationship ensued. In essence, they felt like they got their son back.

WHY WE MAKE ASSUMPTIONS

Why do we make assumptions at all?

Assumptions are rooted in our struggle for survival. Our ancestors, over thousands of generations and millions of years, had to survive long enough to have children. They had to survey millions of data points in their lives and come to decisions quickly that would allow them to survive and pass on their genes. Is that rustling sound the wind, or a tiger in the grass? Is that person's expression friendly or threatening? Is that tribe dangerous or cooperative? Split-second decisions around such questions, made over millions of years, determined who survived and passed on their genes. Over that time, humans developed the instinct that allowed them to assess a situation very quickly. Just as a cat held upside down and dropped will flip itself over and land on its feet—even if it has never done that before—we humans jump to quick conclusions that, historically, were the most likely to save our lives.

When we are in relationships or face the opportunity to make connections, we unconsciously start from our most basic, foundational instinct, which is to determine if someone is a friend or foe. Is this person good for me? Are they bad for me? Am I going to get hurt? We have a lot of mechanisms to protect us from harm, and not just physical harm. We want protection from emotional harm, too. Emotional harm feels just as dangerous to us as physical harm because our fear of emotional harm was developed when we were in infancy. As infants, we knew instinctively that emotional harm (which arose from fear of our losing our parents' care and protection) was truly a matter of life or death. Infants and small children are unavoidably dependent on parents for their very survival.

A parent who ignored us, or was cruel to us, was a parent who could mean the end of us.

Today, you can say that assumptions are tools that allow us to use less energy and fewer analytics to make decisions. We make assumptions in order to avoid repeating the same complex analysis over and over. All things being equal, assumptions speed up our decision making. Keeping brain space open and available is a way to remain vigilant for the next threat and stay alive. Assumptions are an efficient way to do that.

Because our innate tendency to make assumptions is so powerful, we might easily imagine that a certain person might be dangerous to us. Imagination, after all, is much more powerful than our senses. Our senses are quite limited. Birds, bees, and butterflies can see ultraviolet light spectra that we can't see. Dogs and whales and bats can hear frequencies we can't hear. Our senses are very, very limited, and with those limited senses we have to survive. Consequently, we combine the limited inputs of our senses with our instincts to create assumptions that help us survive a world that, for millions of years, was physically very threatening. It's only in the last few decades and centuries that, for most people, the world has become substantially less threatening. That's no time at all in terms of evolutionary change, and our brains haven't caught up. That is to say, our instinctual habits were formed over millions of years, and there is no way that they can be reset to be entirely appropriate to respond to our modern world.

When our senses are unable to provide all the information we need, we use our imagination to fill in the blanks. Doing so has often allowed us a deeper understanding of the truth. For instance, for a long time, humans thought the earth was flat and the sun revolved around it—that's what our senses told us, so we assumed that was correct. Eventually, human imagination (along with science) thought up a different, more accurate way of constructing reality, which was an extraordinary achievement in the face of what our senses told us, and a testament to the power of imagination.

Our intelligence has allowed us to develop many tools to demonstrably prove the things we once only imagined: the Earth does revolve around the sun, there are spectra of light and sound beyond what we can see and hear, and so on. Likewise, we've imagined a lot of things that are incorrect. We imagined that we could sail west from Spain directly to India. We imagined that lightning and thunder were the sounds of Gods fighting.

As a species, we have used our collective observations, our collective tools, and our collective imaginations to make progress toward a greater understanding of what is real. At the same time, we've sometimes gone out over the precipice in directions that are incorrect. We can't just assume that we've got it right. As the bumper sticker says, "Don't Believe Everything You Think." When Galileo suggested the earth revolved around the sun, he was chastised and persecuted by those who insisted they knew what was right. We may tell ourselves we don't make mistakes like that anymore, but we do. Any certainty to the contrary is short-sighted and often incorrect.

ASSUMPTIONS MAY MISLEAD US

Human beings assume all kinds of things that, upon examination, turn out to be wrong, or at the very least questionable.

At least in our Western culture, we live by so many absurd assumptions that it is no wonder that we have a bit of a hard time finding contentment. Here are some lightning-round examples of assumptions that, if you think about them in some depth, you may recognize as dubious if not outright wrong:

- We assume that smiling is good, and frowning is bad.
- We assume that having the same marriage our whole lives is good, but that getting a divorce is bad.
- We assume that it is better to be a more developed country than it is to be a less-developed country.
- We assume that it is better to be happy than sad.
- We assume that running fast is better than running slow.
- We assume that it is better to be rich than poor.
- We assume it is better to live in a big house than a small one.
- We assume that life is better than death.
- We assume that it's better to be young than old.

- We assume that a day where we get a lot done is better than one where we do not get a lot done.
- We assume that it is better to be productive than lazy.
- We assume teaching kids about math, English, and history is important, but that teaching about art, love, relationships, and nutrition is less important.
- We assume lumber has more value than a living tree.
- We assume some weather is "bad weather" and some weather is "good weather."
- We assume it is better to be the winner than it is to be the loser.
- We assume it is better to be the best in the world than the sixth best in the world.
- We assume that winning the lottery will make us happy.
- We assume that certainty is better than uncertainty.
- We assume that it is better for a third grader to read at an eighth-grade level than at a third-grade level.
- We assume that comfort is better than struggle.
- We assume we know what is good and what is bad.
- We assume that other people can make us happy.

Let's look at a few of these assumptions more deeply.

We assume that if a marriage ends, it was a "failed marriage." But when someone's life ends, do we call it a "failed life"? When a president leaves his second term in office, was it then a "failed presidency"? Why do we limit a president to two terms? So that the country gets fresh new ideas and leadership, and no one gets too much power over the people. Could the same logic apply to some marriages, too? Couldn't some "successful" marriages similarly not go on forever? I am not suggesting that marriages shouldn't last, of course. I am questioning the notion that marriages, once ended, were somehow an automatic "failure."

We assume that it is better to be a more developed country than it is to be a less-developed country. But developed countries are often the ones with more pollution per capita, more psychological problems, more depression, less open space, nature, and wilderness, and more parking lots.

We assume that it is better for a third-grade child to read at the eighth-grade level than the third-grade level. We are concerned that our children, if they do not get good enough grades, will "fall behind" the other kids. But what does that mean to "fall behind"? Are we actually in a race? And if we are, what is the finish line? Death? If the finish line is death, isn't it an advantage to fall behind?

We assume that comfort is better than struggle, and we work to create a society with less struggle. Yet when you do something to lessen someone's struggle, you are weakening them and taking away their opportunity to become wiser, more capable and more content. Is that what we should be doing? Don't the best athletes in the world obtain their elite status precisely through struggle?

Perhaps one of the biggest assumptions we make is that other people can make us happy. Our culture promotes this idea relentlessly. As kids we were raised on fairy tales about girls finding Prince Charming and "living happily ever after," or boys finding the "perfect girl to make them happy." Girls in particular were taught that if they just got "the one" to the altar, their life would be bliss. Popular culture—pop songs, movies, romance novels—want men and women alike to believe that they can be happy if only they pair up with the right person. Is that true? Is it fair for anyone to put that kind of pressure on another person?

Perhaps this is the reason that many people make finding the one person who is going to "make them happy" a major life goal. But it is impossible for something or someone to make you happy, for a few reasons. First, happiness can't come from the outside. It arises from within. Second, happiness is fleeting and temporary. It is not a permanent state of being. After all, if you lose a loved one, will you be happy at that moment? Would you even want to be happy at that moment? When you are contemplating the difficulties in our world, such as the mass extinction of species, or the death of thousands in wars around the world, do you want to feel happy about that? Would that be appropriate? Would that be a healthy reaction to a tragedy? Isn't it logical and even respectable to feel sadness when we see other beings in our world who are suffering?

We often seem to place responsibility for our well-being (or lack thereof) onto other people. But is that where we want to find our sense of well-being? Do we want to cede that level of power over our well-being to others? We assume people can make us happy, and that people can make us unhappy. We say things like, "I wouldn't be angry if you hadn't done that," or, "You really hurt me," or, "You really piss me off." All of these statements place the source of our well-being with someone else, which essentially implies that we are a victim of others. Is that healthy? Is that really true?

With practice, we can understand that we are not a victim and that we alone are responsible for our well-being. We can begin to understand that others are not responsible for our actions or feelings, although other people's actions may certainly trigger difficult feelings or sensations inside us. But the key understanding here is that often our difficult feelings and sensations, while potentially triggered by others, are really our own. They emanate from our own internal psychological issues.

If we want to find our true power, then we need to stop believing we are a victim of other people or the world around us. To accomplish this, we can become more aware of how we tend to feel when we encounter certain kinds of stimulus from the world outside, or from people we interact with. For instance, I might sit across from my book editor and talk. If he doesn't say anything to me, just looks at me and listens, I might start to tell myself, "He thinks I'm stupid." He might actually be genuinely listening and thinking, "Monty's on a roll," but that's not the story I'm telling myself. I'm telling myself, "I must be stupid." I could say to him, "You make me feel stupid when you look at me like that." But he doesn't *make* me feel that at all—I may feel stupid, but it's not because of him. It's something triggered inside of me. Wouldn't it be helpful if I chose to locate the source of my own happiness within myself, so that I could take responsibility for it? Wouldn't that be a much healthier way to live my life?

Taking a close look at our many assumptions is a powerful way to begin to question our current world view. This is important to do, since this world view guides all of our decisions, and deeply impacts how we live our lives. In fact, our collective world view as a species is the root cause for tens of thousands of incorrect decisions we are making, as a species, every day. If our view is that the only good moments in our lives are the happy moments, we will likely judge moments of struggle, sadness, or hardship negatively. But struggle is a necessary ingredient to feeling happiness. If we believe that the only purpose of the present moment is to get us to a more interesting future, we will not appreciate or fully experience the present moment. But the present moment is the only one we actually live in, or experience! It is the only moment that is real. Literally, it is the only reality!

By learning to question our elaborate matrix of incorrect assumptions, we can live a more powerful and healthy existence, make better decisions, and live on this planet in a healthy and harmonious way. If we blindly assume that our current, incorrect views are accurate, then change is very unlikely. Therefore, questioning, and the curiosity that powers such questioning, is of critical importance to the improvement of our lives.

For example, many people assume that being rich makes us happy. But when you study the subject, and ask a lot of questions, you may find that the "being rich" part is not really at the heart of what makes some rich people happy. What do I mean by this?

Well, working hard at something meaningful to you tends to provide a lot of satisfaction, and doing so also tends to increase your monetary wealth. Finding a way to help other people, either by providing a service that they need, or creating a product that improves their lives, is very satisfying and also tends to increase your wealth. Bringing your best skill and attention to something you are doing tends to bring you into a close relationship with the present moment, and this is very gratifying, and also tends to increase your wealth. Doing something that you really love is enriching, and therefore you tend to do it very well, which tends to increase your wealth. In other words, I believe that wealth is not the thing that makes people happy, but instead, wealth is often a symptom of a life lived in the present, with focus and attention and hard work at something one cares about deeply, which also tends to help others. This opinion is supported by the many studies that show that earned wealth is correlated with happiness, but that inherited wealth is not.

It is also supported by studies that find that lottery winners are often not happier after winning the lottery.

The point is that, without looking more deeply, we might just assume that wealth makes us happy, and miss the key point that many of the characteristics and habits of some of the people *who end up wealthy* are actually what makes them happy, and wealth is simply one side effect, or manifestation, of these habits and characteristics. In this case, the assumption that wealth makes one happy might very well prevent someone from understanding the root causes of a life well lived, which ironically might even interfere with the attainment of their goal of being wealthy!

Challenging assumptions is a way of getting closer to understanding the truth. It enables us to leave behind fantasy in favor of the freshness of reality. It opens us up to learning the magical truth of the universe. It enables us to learn thousands of lessons that are always available in the world around us.

One key to our growth, therefore, is to become aware of our assumptions and allow ourselves to question whether they are accurate. To accept that maybe our old assumptions aren't helpful. This, in turn, allows us to question, be curious, and be open to what is true. We can bring fresh questions and observations to the world around us. We allow our mind to open, and to learn from our experience.

CHAPTER 6

Dysfunction

As we grow into adulthood, we tend to mature in many ways. We grow more capable of navigating some of life's challenges, learn to fend for ourselves, take care of our needs and tolerate minor discomforts and injustices without over-reacting. But as we reach adulthood, we also tend to hang on to some of our young behaviors well past the time that they serve us.

We tend to be good at outwardly demonstrating visible signs of maturation, such as trading our diapers in for underwear and removing training wheels from our bicycles. But there are many less visible habits and behaviors that we hang on to. Many of these behaviors, when carried into adulthood, become dysfunctional. By dysfunctional, I mean behavior that may have made sense or served us well as infants and toddlers, but which may no longer be appropriate as adults. Such dysfunctions, if they run unchecked, begin to interfere with a life of greater awareness, growth, discovery, and freedom.

Earlier in this book, I described how I learned to please my father by reading his moods and deciding what actions I could take that would most effectively lead to his acceptance. I did this because as a very young child, I was afraid that if I didn't please him, he might not support me, and this could endanger my survival. As infants and young children, we quickly learn techniques that ensure we get the support we need. Acting as I did was NOT dysfunctional at the time. In fact, my actions were entirely logical and appropriate for a youngster trying to ensure his survival. Now that I am fifty-six, if I continue to habitually repeat these same efforts with the people in my life, such behavior becomes dysfunctional. For instance, if I continue to spend all of my effort trying to please people around me, I may sacrifice my own integrity and my own needs in an effort to gain favor with others. This isn't just hypothetical. I still have a very strong tendency to want to please others, and sometimes I do this to my own detriment. The downside is that this can cause me to feel resentful when my needs are not met. Or I may feel like I am being taken advantage of, when really I am the one giving myself away.

We might find a simpler example by looking at a baby crying. It is entirely appropriate for a baby to cry when he is hungry, overly tired, cold, or in pain. It is the most effective way that a baby can attract the needed attention from his parents (or whoever is near) to solve his problem. But, if at fifty-six years old someone cries every time they are hungry, we would say that such behavior is dysfunctional. It is no longer the most appropriate way to get their needs met. At fifty-six, an adult has many other skills and abilities by which they can stave off their hunger.

Children crave attention from their parents. Through millions of years of evolution, we have developed instincts that equate receiving attention from our parents with survival. If, as infants, we didn't get such attention, we wouldn't have survived. This desire for attention from parents is so strong that children go to significant lengths to get it. While children might prefer to get positive attention, if they cannot attract positive attention, they'll settle for negative attention, since any attention means survival. The worst-case scenario is to be ignored. Forgotten. Historically, this meant death.

One of my friends has a son who started acting up at a young age, and my friend wondered why. His daughter got lots of attention for being, essentially, a goody-goody. She behaved well, always did what her parents asked, did well in school, and was seen by both her parents as a "dream child." His son had a very tough time getting attention for being good, since his sister had the market cornered in the goody-goody department. Since he wasn't able to attract much positive attention, he started acting up. When he acted up, he got lots of attention in the form of discipline, criticism, yelling, and various forms of drama. While many parents would assume that such negative attention (like discipline or punishment) would cause their son to improve his behavior, usually the opposite is true. The reason for this is that instinct caused the son to know that attention, even if negative, meant survival. A lack of attention meant death.

When a child who got a lot of attention from acting up becomes an adult, they may have developed a habit. They will likely find themselves continuing to equate acting up with survival. They may be quicker to get into arguments and generally be more comfortable with conflict and negativity since these mannerisms were an effective currency during their formative childhood years. In other words, such a person may actually subconsciously cultivate negativity as an adult, since they subconsciously believe that this is the best way to ensure their survival.

If we are open to exploring our own dysfunction, it can be fascinating to look at the behaviors that we cultivated that were most successful to our childhood effort to get attention and care. When I do that, I discover many things. My brother was the child who acted out. When I came along, I found that I got a lot more of what I needed by pleasing my parents. To this day, I am very uncomfortable if anyone is disappointed in me, and my brother really doesn't care much if someone is disappointed in him. I found ways to please my father, and my brother found ways to challenge him. Both strategies worked in that we both got attention. You might say that my strategy was the better one, since it is based on being "good" and "nice" and "kind." But that view is overly simplistic. My brother enjoys a freedom that I don't enjoy. He is free to ignore what others think of him. I feel somehow required to please them. It can be exhausting. And even though I am aware of it, I can still feel the pull of the old habit I learned so many years ago. Habits learned during our formative years are very hard to break.

If we open our minds and question our behaviors as adults, we may find that many of our behaviors are no longer most appropriate to the circumstances we encounter. The first step to gaining freedom from these old habits is just to become aware of them. Be careful here: if we choose to label behaviors as "stupid" or "bad," then we are merely strengthening our ego, which is unhelpful to our ability to awaken. The ego likes to judge and label things, including behaviors. The most effective way to work on changing our behaviors is to first bring aware-ness and notice when we continue to act in accordance with old habits that may not be so appropriate to our adult lives.

DEFENSIVENESS

Another obstacle that interferes with healthy connections with others is our tendency to become defensive. People become defensive when their ego feels threatened. In other words, when something threatens the ego, the ego feels diminished, and this feeling ignites a sense of panic for the ego, which above all does not want to feel diminished. A typical response is to become defensive, and often what follows is some sort of aggressive response. If someone is completely present—in other words, spiritually awake at the moment that they encounter something threatening—they will not become defensive. The reason for this is that the truth needs no defense. Put differently, someone who is spiritually awake would not feel that there is a "self" that needs defending. They would not become defensive.

If someone calls Niagara Falls a tiny, weak little stream, that does not change the amount of water going over the falls. If someone tells a mountain that it is a prairie, the mountain doesn't lose any altitude or majesty. Likewise, if you insult someone who is awake to their essential nature, they don't feel a need to defend against the insult, since they are aware that the insult has nothing to do with them. It does not define them. It does not, by virtue of being said, make anything more or less true than before it was said. If we hear ourselves say, "I can't believe that person just insulted me! Oh my God! That's outrageous," we can be sure our ego is in control. When we are spiritually awake, we are aware of and in touch with the truth, which in this case is that the insult has no effect on who we are. The insult is therefore not threatening.

Looking for moments when we feel defensive, therefore, is helpful to better understanding the presence of our ego. What we will find is that when we are defensive, our ego is activated. If we can remain aware, we may notice that our defensive reaction is not helpful. When we are busy defending ourselves, we are not actually present in the moment, and we are not available to have a real connection with others, or the world around us. We are, in such moments, spiritually asleep.

WHEN YOU FEEL DEFENSIVE

If you are interacting with someone and you feel yourself becoming defensive, this is a precious opportunity from a spiritual growth perspective. During such moments, if we can remember to ask, "What am I about to defend? Does it need defending? Why is it important to defend it?" we can learn a great deal. We will notice our defensiveness, which will manifest as a need to correct someone, or explain ourselves. When we notice this tendency, we can become aware of our ego in action. When we are still confusing ourselves to believe that we *are* our ego, we will often feel a strong need to defend ourselves. This need will inevitably cause us to argue unnecessary points, seek credit even where credit is irrelevant, try to show we were right when it doesn't really matter, and so forth.

Defensiveness usually kicks in when we are challenged in a way that triggers an insecurity we are already suffering from. If someone says, "Hey Shorty," to me, I am not going to feel defensive. I am six foot four, and I do not harbor insecurities about my height. I don't need to defend that. If someone says, "You were a lousy CEO," that's more complicated. It might trigger a defensive reaction. I was a CEO for twenty-three years. There were times I believe I did things well, and times I didn't. In my heart of hearts, I probably understand the nuances of my performance. But perhaps I've felt the need to create a fantasy in my head about how I was always a great CEO. That's my ego at work, and since the ego is always insecure, and always seeking to build itself up bigger and stronger, it will not rest and simply accept that "it is what it is," but instead will feel a need to support my internal narrative that I was "a great CEO." When someone says, "You were a lousy CEO," that assertion may trigger my ego to defend itself to protect my egoic fantasy.

But the truth doesn't need defense. If my ego were not engaged around this idea that I was a great CEO, my response to criticism would be very different. I would not feel the need to defend. I would rest in the comfort that my record is what it is. If someone said, "You were a lousy CEO," I might either not respond, or I might say, "Aha. I hope you weren't overly affected by my shortcomings." I could leave it alone. I could rest in a state of peace, even in the wake of such a remark. There would be no need for me to pout, suffer, or engage in any psychological drama. Imagine the amount of energy I'd save!

I know you are probably thinking that such a comment would make almost anyone feel bad or trigger a need to defend. You're right! But the reason for this is NOT that any defense is needed or warranted. The reason, instead, is that most of us spend most of our time in an egoic state. Just being aware of this is a wonderfully powerful spiritual exercise, as watching for our defensiveness can teach us a lot about our state of presence or lack thereof. It can teach us whether we are operating mostly from our ego, or mostly from an awareness of what is actually real in the moment. If we are truly present and spiritually awake, we can actually relax in the face of criticism, and remain capable of connecting and learning. But if we are not present, not spiritually awake, then we will inevitably become mired in the need to defend ourselves. There will be a lot of mental noise, suffering, and unnecessary mental turbulence. Such is the way of the ego. This is another reason why it is worth waking up!

THE EGO DEFENDS IDENTITY

There's so much knowledge and growth to be gained through this kind of examination, but unfortunately, our ego is set up to defend against such growth. We tend to become most defensive about exactly those things that our ego has assimilated as being part of our identity: part of the story about ourselves that our ego tells us is who we are. The story about ourselves that we want to represent to others. When this ego narrative is threatened, as it is by a perceived insult ("You were a lousy CEO"), our ego launches into action before we can even give any consideration as to why we're threatened. This reactivity results when we are spiritually asleep. Unaware of the truth. By becoming aware of the cause of our tendency to react, we can start to learn a lot about the flavor of our ego, and also about areas where we are least comfortable feeling our vulnerability. In other words, the stronger our desire to defend, the more we are avoiding some vulnerability that we are not comfortable feeling. By coming to learn, understand, and accept such vulnerabilities, we can begin to understand ourselves better. It is by saying "yes" to the reality of our psychological makeup, that we can begin to actually know what is true about ourselves. When we get to this point, we grow patient and compassionate with ourselves and can begin to allow the present moment to exist without the need to defend. From this place, we can grow. We can change. We can be present. We can live in truth and feel the warm and accepting embrace of love which results from an acceptance of what is.

This exercise of exploring the vulnerabilities that we're most hesitant to accept is a way of discovering places where your ego is trying to compensate for what it believes are shortcomings in your life, background, or history. Asking, "Why do I need to defend?" opens a window to allow you to find the drama you are creating, which in turn allows you a chance to begin to relax into reality and accept what is.

If someone accused me of being a bad father, I might get defensive about that, especially if I've added "good father" to my ego's story about "who I am." When I feel the defensiveness arising in me, if I can intervene and ask, "Why do I feel such a deep need to defend myself?" there is a lot I can learn. Perhaps the reason for my defensiveness is that I equate being a bad father with being somehow unworthy of love, which triggers my unresolved childhood fears of abandonment. There is tremendous value in allowing myself to experience the raw, painful vulnerability of this fear of abandonment. To stay with this empty and painful sensation, and to realize that it will not kill me, or even harm me, allows the negativity and pain to gradually dissipate. There is real power in realizing that, as an adult, I can now tolerate such difficult feelings, and relax. The trouble is that the very act of defending—which sends me into a debate about when I've been a "good" or "bad" father— immediately prevents the kind of inner exploration which might actually allow me to discover my own vulnerability, which I am defending against feeling. Only by becoming one with this vulnerability is it possible to awaken. In this case, launching a defense would've prevented me from accepting my vulnerability, and feeling the peace of a union with the truth of the present moment.

Unpacking your own defensiveness, and thus becoming familiar with your inner vulnerabilities, is a tool by which you can observe your ego in action and begin to wake up to the difference between your ego and your true nature. You can begin to replace reactions and compulsive defensiveness with awareness and an understanding of reality. Instead of reacting, you can act with intention and purpose. You can begin to better align yourself with the truth. The alternative is to remain in an egoic state. To remain spiritually asleep. The trouble is that, by remaining asleep, you'll miss out on the freshness, magic, mystery, and beautiful potential you have to live this life to its fullest.

EXPLORE DISCOMFORT

Doing this work has helped me learn not to avoid uncomfortable sensations, and instead to lean into short-term pain in order to reap the rewards of heightened awareness and wakefulness.

This same desire to live in harmony with reality which drives me to seek a higher level of self-awareness also drives me to seek a higher level of authenticity in my relationships with others. I know that the uncomfortable feeling I get when something isn't right between me and someone else is not something I should ignore, but instead is something I should explore. I know I have to confront discomfort, even if it makes me nervous and uncomfortable, because by doing so my relationships with others become more authentic and deepen.

Someone described taking this kind of action as "leaving no crumbs on the table." A crumb is a little thing in a relationship that bothers you. It could be the way your boss sometimes reads over your shoulder when you are writing on your computer, which makes you nervous. Or the way your partner loads the dishwasher, which seems all wrong. Or the way your sister makes little comments about the décor in your home that feel like tiny criticisms of your taste.

Most of us choose to leave the crumbs. We don't want to have the uncomfortable conversation. We instead distract ourselves with small talk, or trivia, or gossip, or perhaps we even argue about things we do not really care about to avoid the real issues that have built up. All of this erodes intimacy. It erodes our attraction to someone. It breeds resentment. Over time the crumbs keep piling up and get harder and harder to clean up. Eventually, we don't even remember what caused the mess, which makes solving it, and returning to intimacy, all the more difficult. As more and more crumbs stick to the table, they're harder to dislodge even if you try, and often people just give up. It is better to just "clean as you go" and have the courage to dive into the truth, even when it is uncomfortable.

In order to keep your relationships clean and crumb-free, find and hold your vulnerability. Within that holding of your vulnerability, find the elements that are uniquely yours—in other words, your insecurities. Call it what you like; what matters is that you identify the vulnerabilities that you are trying not to feel, the things that allow others to push your buttons. Once you find those vulnerabilities, and embrace and accept them, you can begin to develop more confidence, react less, and become capable of a much deeper relationship with yourself and others.

CHAPTER 7

Labels

M ost of us have a habit that is so pervasive that we are not even aware of it. I am talking about the habit of labeling things.

By labeling, I mean that we tend to quickly label the people and objects in our lives when we see them, and by doing so, assume that we know what we need to know about them. Labels like "good" and "bad" are rooted in deeper assumptions about survival that once looked like "don't run" or "run like hell." We want to name things quickly because naming them lets us quickly reach a conclusion and take action. Our brains want to understand, label and file something as good/bad, dangerous/ not dangerous, and so on, without working through a lot of complexity. Out on the prehistoric savannah, sometimes we didn't have the time for such complexity.

But labels tend to limit our ability to truly understand the world around us. By labeling things, we essentially turn off our powers of deeper observation. We terminate our analysis. We do not allow ourselves to witness the depth and uniqueness that each experience offers us. This causes us to remain spiritually asleep. But it also interferes with our ability to connect with other people.

Labels stifle curiosity. "Good" and "bad" are unhelpful labels that cause people to make a judgment that, once made, tends to limit them from pursuing a deeper and more helpful analysis. Choosing not to believe in "good" and "bad" can allow you to think more deeply and to avoid making premature judgments that would limit your full consideration of an issue. Likewise, "right" and "wrong" are also unhelpful, because once we decide something is right or wrong, it again tends to shut down any further analysis.

What do these words really mean?

Here's an easy example. We might think ice cream is "good." We like the way it tastes. We like the way it makes us feel. We like the social aspect of going out for ice cream with our family. But if ice cream is slowly killing us by making us obese, or diabetic, is it really "good"? Or is it "bad"?

When we are trying to describe deeper concepts like "God" "love" or "enlightenment" we need to understand the fundamental inadequacy of words. We need to use words simply as guardrails, and understand that they are not precise, when we are describing these more complex issues. Certain words are more dangerous than others because they purport to be more powerful than they deserve to be. The word "chair" is not particularly dangerous since people seldom use it to pin down the listener's understanding. It is rarely used irresponsibly. But other words are more dangerous, since they tend to conjure up judgments or assumptions that are often, if not usually, at least largely incorrect.

For instance, the words "good" and "bad" are very dangerous, since they are almost always used in a way that is at least partially misleading. As such, using them usually limits, rather than advances, the true understanding of the listener. These words are more destructive than helpful to communication, and therefore tend to interfere with our connection with others. For example, if we say "that guy is a really bad person" we are almost certainly wrong. This is true because no one is all bad, nor is anyone all good. The words "good" and "bad" are therefore inherently misleading when used to describe a person. Now if we want to convey that a bottle of milk has become rancid, we are probably safe saying, "this milk has gone bad." The first example is an example of an irresponsible way of using the label "bad" and the second example is a more responsible example of using the label "bad."

Using more skilled and careful words that are less judgmental and more revealing of helpful facts tends to foster more effective communication. For instance, it is problematic and unhelpful to say, "Syria is a bad country." It is not so problematic or unhelpful to say that "Syria is a country that has within its borders terrorist training camps." The former is merely a negative judgment. The latter is a potentially helpful statement of fact.

There are other words commonly used to describe people that pretend to be highly descriptive but tend to be at least partially inaccurate. For instance, if we say "that guy is a Republican," such a statement carries with it a broad array of assumptions about the person, many of which are likely incorrect, since people tend not to fall neatly into broad detailed categories. Other labels like "fascist" or "liberal" or "tyrant" likewise need to be used carefully, since they purport to describe a broad array of characteristics about someone, and it is usually the case that the person described will not fit so neatly into the picture that is painted by using the label.

Certain words are more communicative than problematic. Some are more problematic than communicative. Our task is to use language in a way that is more communicative and less problematic. Examples of the less communicative and more problematic words are words like "Republican," "Democrat," "woke," and "progressive." Examples of the words that tend to be more communicative than problematic are words like "above," "below," "up," and "down." Usually, simpler words are less likely to create misunderstandings.

Because they have power, we need to use words carefully. We also need to understand that certain words tend to limit understanding as much as they advance understanding, if not more so, and thus are best avoided. We should be suspicious of words that tend to be used to oversimplify or "pin down" a complex person or subject, as they will more likely create misunderstanding. So, we will be best served by using such words sparingly and carefully. If we fail to realize this, then we may unwittingly be communicating poorly with other people, and this can interfere with our connection to them. Understanding this is a great place to start to make a change in yourself toward better human connection. You can see how much energy you waste judging and labeling people and the world around you in a way that prevents you from having an authentic experience, and begin to understand how this interferes with your spiritual journey.

For example, you wake up in the morning and right away you judge the weather—is it a good day, or a bad day? But the weather just is. It's neither good nor bad. Labeling it "good" or "bad" interferes with our ability to simply experience what is. I am not saying you should stop saying, "It's a beautiful day," but I am suggesting that it is useful to be aware that when you label this day beautiful, then you will likely label another day not beautiful. Be aware that as long as there is a judgment, then you are not fully allowing the uniqueness of the present moment. You could experience the rainiest day and it could be the best day of your life. There's no reason it couldn't. It's not a good day or a bad day because of the weather. It's just a day.

EVEN DEATH MAY BE MISLABELED

When a baby is born, we celebrate and send flowers, balloons, cards, and gifts. But when someone dies, we send condolences. We cry and mourn. Does this make sense? Is a birth better than a death? It is very worthwhile to challenge our assumptions and prejudices in this way.

We are born into a world where we struggle, feel painful emotions and unwanted sensations, cry, suffer, and eventually grow old, feel our body slowly fall into dysfunction and weakness, and die. Of course, we also have great and magical times along the way. But no one gets through this life without pain, fear, anxiety, heartbreak, discomfort, and suffering. Some may reach an enlightened state, and they may not suffer any more. But even they continue to feel pain, sadness, discomfort, and other feelings and sensations that most of us find distasteful and not preferable. (Enlightened people feel feelings and sensations, but do not reject such sensations anymore, therefore they do not suffer. Suffering is a choice, whereas pain is a condition we all must face. Suffering is, essentially, the mental rejection of pain.)

Death is a little tougher to feel positively about, because very few (if any) survive to write about it. A few claim to have "died" and come back. In this regard, we often hear stories about seeing light, beauty, and having a sense of complete bliss before "coming back to life." Most of the world's religions promise a state of bliss after our worldly existence ends. Most describe some sort of heaven, or peace, or tranquility. Of course, some religions say that certain unworthy people who have lived life improperly or in a "sinful" way will "go to hell." I think this idea of a "hell" that awaits you when life ends is absurd and nonsensical. I believe that there is no such thing as "hell" after death. During life? Maybe. Hell is a state of dysfunction, and a lot of us live in dysfunction every day.

At any rate, it doesn't make sense to me that what happens after death could be bad. If you will allow me to be a bit light and playful about a subject most are not light about, here are the possibilities that I can think of.

First, let's say that when you die, you cease to exist in any way, shape, or form. You really are "gone." In that case, you do not suffer, hurt, or have anything negative ever happen again. Thus, death is not a negative thing. Those you leave behind may miss you and hurt because of your loss. But it is not bad for the person who dies.

Second, let's say there is a heaven. Complete bliss. Unity with God, as well as everyone you've ever loved and lost. And, if you are one with God, and God loves and knows all people, and protects and cares about them, then you are still with the living too! This sounds wonderful! If this is the case, death is not something negative.

Third, let's say there is a hell. Again, this concept doesn't make sense to me. But if there was one, I suppose then you "deserve" to be there. And if you really deserve to be there, isn't it "good" that you got what you deserve? If you are saying "No! No one deserves that!" then, well, you are thinking like me! If no one truly deserves that, then no decent, loving, all powerful God would send anyone there. So back to the start. The concept doesn't make sense to me.

Fourth, let's say that the body dies, but the soul lives on, becoming one with the universal consciousness, or God. Well, that sounds nice! After all, the body ages, aches, has pain, and needs food, water, and to have its back scratched. Death would do away with those needs. Since the soul would have no body, then the soul could be anywhere it wants to be. In other words, the soul could be in and around the hearts and minds and souls of all the most wonderful people and spirits and animals all at once, and even could be at one with God! How terrific!

Fifth, let's say that when you die you are reborn into another life. Reincarnation. Rebirths mean that you would have "life everlasting." If that is true, then death is truly just a rebirth, and therefore is not something to condole! Instead, let's celebrate that old uncle Billy Bob has been reborn afresh!

The only point I am trying to make with all of this is to say that, since we do not know what happens after death, making the assumption that it is "bad" does not make much sense. None of the possibilities I outlined above seem "bad." Logically, then, it makes little sense to be so sure that death is "bad." Yet death is almost universally feared and thought to be negative. Why?

Really having to think through something like this takes effort. Most of us prefer to just make quick judgments, like good, bad, right, wrong, because that's what we've evolved to do. The problem with this approach is that this tendency to label things before truly understanding leads to misunderstandings, xenophobia, racism, classism, sexism, and even genocide. (Once enough people believed Hitler was "good" for Germany, many accepted what he did without question. This happened in Rwanda, Bosnia, and Myanmar, too.)

QUESTIONING LABELS

In early 2021, I contracted coronavirus. Fortunately, my infection was very mild, and lasted only three days. When people heard I had it, they said, "Oh, no! That sucks." But in reality those three days were really fun for me. Since the illness made me feel a bit low energy, but not very ill, I allowed myself to relax and watch a few old golf tournaments on a very comfortable couch. I found the whole experience very satisfying and even enriching. Was it "bad" that I contracted COVID-19? Well, not for me. I actually rather enjoyed my time. Of course, I am not trying to make light of coronavirus generally —I am aware that many others have suffered terribly and even died from it.

The point is to take note of how often in your life you judge something as good or bad. Judgment is always ego-based because it's about ranking ourselves or our experiences against others. Judgment and labeling are based entirely on assumptions—that some things are bad, and others are good, some worse, others better—when in reality we know very little, if anything, about what is "good" or "bad" for us. (That rainy day could be the best thing that ever happened to you!) When you're judging others, there is an inherent assumption that you know what is best. But the reality is, you cannot know that. For this reason, whenever we're judging ourselves or someone else, we're not at our best. We are operating from a place of ego, on assumptions that are likely incorrect.

If we can learn to avoid labeling, especially in cases where we feel initial discomfort, remain curious, and perhaps ask questions that allow us to seek a connection with another human being who is going through something that seems painful and difficult, there is room for a deep connection, and perhaps even a magical moment. The way we can stop labeling is to simply observe the people and world around us with curiosity, and accept what we see. We can substitute awareness for judgment, and just witness people, animals, trees, birds, sounds, and smells for what they are. When we do this, we live life freshly. We begin to understand what is true and real. We have more presence in our lives. We allow for endless possibilities. This is very enriching. It's a gift not to know if anything in our immediate experience is "good" or "bad" because that not-knowing allows you to live with curiosity, unfolding mystery, and spontaneity.

CHAPTER 8

Lenses

There was a simple experiment I remember from when I was in elementary school. We were provided a simple picture that had lines drawn in a few different colors. Then the teacher handed us little sheets of transparent plastic, one red and one blue. We were told to look at the drawings through these colored plastic sheets and see what happened. When I looked through the red plastic sheet, all of the red lines on the drawing seemed to disappear. When I looked through the blue plastic sheet, all of the blue lines disappeared. This simple experiment provides a good analogy for how all of us see the world. We see some things that others don't, or we see them differently than others do. All of us have lenses that cause us to see the world differently, and that's okay. In fact, it's inevitable.

When we are in a relationship, we cannot help but interpret the other person's behavior based on how we see it through our own lens, which is constructed from our own judgments and biases.

For example, one person might have grown up in a family where people yelled and argued a lot. They didn't bottle things up, but instead got them off their chest. Unwittingly, this person may have developed a belief that this sort of behavior is what a loving family does. They might then assume that if someone really loves them, that they will make a lot of noise and argue a lot.

This person who comes from a loud, argumentative family may later find themselves in a relationship with someone who comes from a family that never argued and saw harsh words as unloving, inelegant, and vile. This other person might have come to believe that a loving family is one where people are quiet, cooperative, and mellow. If they have a problem, they keep it to themselves. The person from the loud family might subconsciously feel unloved by their quiet partner. They might think, "Why are they being so quiet?" Their lens might convince them, "If they really loved me, they'd be more animated. They'd show more passion for me. I don't see the passion." They might develop an insecurity, even though their partner loves them deeply.

The reverse could be happening to the quiet partner. They might think, "God, this person is so loud. That's very threatening." Their lens might cause them to judge their partner's arguing as threatening and unloving. Both parties are operating from assumptions that are incorrect. They both are looking through lenses that create real barriers to understanding and connecting with the other.

SEE YOUR OWN LENSES

The way I perceive the world is different than the way every one of the eight billion other people on this planet perceive it. So is yours. My perception may be similar to some and violently different from others', because everyone's perceptions—what comes through their lens—are based on their experiences and the forces that acted upon them throughout their life, especially their very young life. When we are young, the world is new to us, and we are aware that we need to find a way to survive. What one child feels they need to do to survive might differ greatly from what another child feels they need to do to survive. We are very malleable when we are young. We quickly learn to see and interpret the world in ways that best ensure our survival.

While it is completely natural that all of us see things through different lenses, it can also be the source of a lot of misunderstanding. For instance, my wife and I have often interpreted some of our conversations very differently. Sometimes, she is hurt by what I have said, when I feel that I've been very friendly. The same goes the other way. What we have learned through our exploration of some of our disagreements is that she tends to care a great deal about the words that come out of my mouth, with less regard for my tone, and I care about the tone with which she speaks, with less regard for her words. This is a bit of an issue, because with people I am close to, I tend to be loose and playful with words, relying mostly on my tone to convey whether I am serious or kidding. This makes perfect sense to me, because I believe that someone's tone is a much better indication of what they are really communicating than their words. But often my wife seizes on particular words that I've used, which may not be representative of what I was really trying to communicate. Now that I know how she listens, I can be more skilled in how I communicate with her by choosing my words more carefully.

The key is to learn the differences in how you, and others with whom you interact, view things. This way, you develop a broader understanding about potential sources of misunderstanding, which improves your ability to communicate. One of the best tools by which to accomplish this is curiosity. If you remain curious about others, you will notice how they experience reality. You will better understand their experience, and how it differs from yours. Once you're aware that you're looking at things through your own lens, you can observe whether you are perceiving things differently than others. You can watch your observations lead to certain conclusions and begin to develop awareness as to how those conclusions are affected by your own biases and experiences. Specifically, you can begin to develop awareness of old habits rooted in your childhood desire to survive.

This practice is difficult, though, because it is often hard to stay present when something offends us, because more often than not, we tend to react to the events in the world around us before we even get a chance to slow down and be present. We are not really even conscious, but rather are "caught up in the moment." We then respond to external stimuli before we even allow room for awareness to arise. If the first step is understanding that we have a lens, and the second step is understanding that we habitually react to external stimuli, the third step is to learn to observe and begin to understand our tendency to be reactive, and to explore the reasons behind our reactions. We then can begin to see that our reactions are based on inaccurate assumptions and are no longer appropriate.

This practice is very difficult because reactions happen instantly but gaining an awareness about things takes time. Learning about our own lenses (better understanding how our unique outlook is affecting our connection with another person) requires us to look backward after we have had a strong reaction. Only by looking backward and training ourselves to see how our reactions may have been unnecessary or inappropriate can we begin to become aware of how our unique lens is impacting our connection. Once we do that, we can train ourselves not to react, but instead to create a moment of space before a reaction.

I got a solid reminder about this subject when my in-laws came to visit us from England. My wife and I got in a small argument about something minor, and I kept wanting to talk it through with her. She just wanted to forget about it, let it go, and go relax on the back patio with her mother. Her desire to let it go triggered feelings in me that she didn't care enough to talk it through. A few minutes later, her mother came into the room, and gave me some advice. "Sometimes things go better if you just let them go, and move on." Soon after, her father and I had a laugh about how English people and American people sometimes had different styles, in that English people often are less apt to discuss feelings, and American people tend to want to talk things out. I soon realized that while I thought wanting to talk things out was a caring act, in my wife's mind, wanting to let them go was a caring act. We had different lenses through which we observed identical facts quite differently. But once I realized that she meant to be caring, and once she realized that I meant to be caring, we both felt good, and the argument vanished. The key now will be to retain awareness of this knowledge to prevent difficult misunderstandings from arising in the first place.

The practice I am describing requires that we learn to notice our reactions before they lead to action. In other words, to feel the reaction begin to rise up in us, become aware of it, and then to interject awareness before we react. In that moment of awareness, there is room for choice. When we are merely reacting, we are not acting with intent, but rather are simply replaying old programs that are often no longer the best way to handle a situation. When we are aware, we can assess how we want to behave in light of the actual situation we find ourselves in.

Once you begin to notice that some of your behaviors result from unconscious reactions, and therefore not from awareness, you can begin to make choices as an adult, responding to the actual circumstances that are in front of you, rather than merely react, using the same techniques that served you in your infancy. In other words, you begin to respond, not react. This practice of developing some space between a stimulus and what you do in response to it gives you choice. You act consciously, rather than compulsively. You bring more intelligence and more awareness to your response, so that your actions are more appropriate.

This practice of creating space between a stimulus and a response is difficult but very helpful. As you engage in the practice, you may notice that a great many of your actions are actually reactions. You may find that much of your time in life is spent acting out the same habitual actions that you've undertaken for years, or even decades. When you see this, you might conclude that your life is not as fresh and new as you deserve it to be. You might find that you are a creature of habit. The trouble is that habitual behavior is not fresh. You are not really living, but instead acting like a complex machine that is preprogrammed to react in certain ways. Continuing in this way is beneath your capability. It means that you will live without making many connections with others that are fresh, new, and exciting.

But by simply becoming aware of your tendency to live habitually, you may learn to challenge some of your habits. You may notice that your habitual behavior is not serving you very well anymore. It is not interesting. It is not genuine. It is not born out of awareness and appreciation for the uniqueness of the present moment. You may realize that each moment of your life is not something to merely navigate, but rather is something to be cherished. Something sacred.

PART III

Love In Action

A woman once told me she developed amazing relation-
ships during transatlantic flights—they seemed almost
deeper and better than the relationships she had with
her friends.

Why was that?

On an airplane, you have no commitment to the person
sitting next to you. If the conversation is going badly, you can
simply read a book or talk to the person sitting on the other side.
In a few hours, you'll separate and likely never see each other
again. There's almost no risk in a relationship like that. Because
you're generally not going to stay in touch, you can open your-
self up to deep connection without really putting anything at
risk. Additionally, a new person is a clean slate: they harbor no
resentment toward you, and few if any preconceived notions
about you. It is a fresh start.

But if you want to develop deeper connections with greater
intimacy, it is necessary to put more on the table.

Deep relationships are hard, but worthwhile: it's nice to be
seen and understood at a deeper level. It's nice to know that
each time you talk you aren't introducing yourself and your work
history. It is nice to skip past the small talk that characterizes
most initial interactions. To have people in your life with whom
you don't always have to start over from the beginning. Such
relationships offer the opportunity to go deeper. To learn more
about yourself. To learn more about others, and more about the
world around you. Deeper relationships are one of the best ways

to gain a greater awareness of oneself and the truth of the world that surrounds us.

No doubt, the "airplane" relationship can be very comforting. It is nice to open up to someone new and cathartic to be with someone who does not have any preconceived notions about who you are. Conversely, deeper, longer-term relationships are almost certainly going to challenge you, even when you are not in the mood to be challenged! Deeper relationships can push you in ways that will tend to cause you to grow, and growing can be uncomfortable. But growth is also our most natural state, and avoiding growth always leads to dysfunction.

Have you heard the saying that "no man is a hero to his wife" (which perhaps is better restated today as "no person is a hero to their partner")? Perhaps it's true that people who know you best will seldom idealize you or hold you in awe. In reality, being a "hero" is not a realistic overall assessment of any of us. Since it is not realistic, it is not true. Since it is not true, it is not something worth basing our long-term efforts on, because if we are to live life to the fullest, and become the best version of ourselves, we have to do so in a way that is true and real. Otherwise, we are living in fantasy.

If we choose to risk knowing our friends and partners more deeply, we have an opportunity to love them in a more complete and more genuine way. By doing so, we also can better understand the world, and awaken to the beautiful, positive, and magical reality of the universe.

This experience of becoming enriched by virtue of a deeper relationship can happen in many areas in our life. For example, when I first moved to Los Angeles from Boulder, Colorado, after finishing college, I didn't like the city at all. I found it big and anonymous and noisy and crowded. I felt like a drop in a huge bucket. I felt meaningless. Small. Helpless. I got a job as an insurance adjuster, and over time had the opportunity to travel throughout the city. As I saw more and more—ugly parts, nice parts, rich parts, poor parts—I began to feel that I knew the place in a deeper way. I began to feel an intimacy with it. As I grew more familiar and more intimate with Los Angeles, I started to find myself warming to it. I began to like it a lot. By virtue of my more complete knowledge of it, I started to find beauty in it. I found merit in the place. It started to feel like home.

Likewise, you might meet someone who initially scares you a little bit. Maybe they question you in ways you haven't been questioned. They challenge you in ways you haven't been challenged. They notice things that perhaps others haven't noticed—things that trigger positive feelings in you, and things that trigger difficult feelings in you: perhaps even leaving you feeling threatened. But the better they get to know you, and the better you get to know them, the more opportunity there is for deeper connection. To really understand their reality. To get to what is real in the relationship. This is simultaneously a bit unsettling at times, and exciting.

In the following chapters I share what I've learned through my own experiences making connections as a business leader, a friend, and a stranger. I don't pretend to be an expert in any of those arenas. I do know what has worked for me, and that is what I share with you.

CHAPTER 9

Professional
Relationships

I spend every July at a lake house in New Hampshire with my friends and family. I fly my small airplane to a little airport and rent a hangar for a month. One summer I forgot to make the reservation. Hangar space was at a premium. So were rental cars. I hadn't arranged for either from the company at the airport that rents hangars and cars to pilots.

A few days before my arrival, I crossed my fingers and called the airport to see if I could get a rental car, and a place to store my plane. Instead of saying, "Hello, Skybright Aviation," the manager, Lee, answered, "Hello, Monty, we've been waiting for your call." Turns out that even though I hadn't called them for almost a year, they had held a rental car and hangar space for me "because we've been expecting you."

There is no doubt that this was amazing customer service. But the truth is that I feel like the people at Skybright are my friends. Now, I don't know these people well, but nonetheless I feel a strong positive connection with them. Each year when I fly in, I give an enthusiastic greeting to Michael, who is usually the one who greets me when I open the door of my plane, and Lee, who manages the place. They are terrific people. We usually haven't spoken since the previous year, when we chatted for a few minutes about this and that. But during our brief conversations we always have a real connection. Michael and Lee *know* me. I am on their minds when they think of who will likely need their services for the summer. They care about me, and I care about them. We share a connection.

The best customer service requires this kind of connection. It requires vulnerability, care, and concern. So do all business relationships.

IT'S MORE
THAN "JUST BUSINESS"

There is a belief in the business world that "business" relationships are and should be less about love than "personal" relationships. The thought is that business relationships might be founded on trust, but not love, because people assume business relationships are different from personal relationships. Business relationships are not expected to merit a deep connection. After all, we've all heard someone say, "It's nothing personal; it's just business."

But this is nonsense.

On the one hand, our whole life has been permeated by love. We learn a thousand sayings like, "Love is what makes the world go round." We click heart symbols on a billion social media images. We sing along to love songs. Every marketing company in the world knows that they can motivate us to buy things through manipulating our desire to be seen, valued, understood, and loved. They try to convince us that we'll be more loved with a Rolex than with a Timex, and more loved with a Ferrari than a Fiat. Everything's about love. Then we go to the workplace and all of a sudden we assume that our relationships with each other shouldn't be based on love. This doesn't make sense.

Business is extremely personal. There is nothing *not* personal about business. Deep connections based on trust, understanding, mutuality of concern, love, and compassion are just as important in a business relationship, if not more important, than a more casual friendship or even, arguably, in a marriage, because business relationships affect every single part of your life. When you're buying a home, which is a very personal and emotional decision, it's a business transaction *and* a personal transaction. When you're talking to your boss about getting a raise, that's a business transaction *and* very personal, because your compensation is going to affect your personal life.

Business relationships may affect a large group of employees or customers or other stakeholders. They may have a huge downstream effect. All of the people affected by a business want to be seen, valued, understood, and loved, so there's absolutely no reason to ever take the attitude of "it's just business."

It's true that many business relationships are not especially deep. But it is also true that most business relationships would be much more advantageous and enriching to all parties concerned if they were based on a deeper connection: if they were based upon care, concern, and even love. Better relationships are critical to every part of our lives.

If you go to buy a car and you establish a connection with the car salesman, you will have a better experience buying your car. Car salesmen sometimes have a reputation for being cheesy, for seeing you as another mark, another chit on their monthly total. If you are treated this way, and you buy a car anyway, that negative experience will carry over into your experience of owning the car. You won't feel as good. Feeling good about a transaction has to do with a number of things. First, you have to trust that it's a good car. But you also have to feel that you were well treated and paid a fair price. That your experience with that salesman felt authentic and real.

If you slow down enough to establish a connection with the salesman, they will feel a connection with you. There will be mutual respect. You'll get a better deal because they'll feel a commitment to help you in a way that's positive and fair. You won't always make a connection every time you try, but you will most of the time. You can empathize with what that salesman is going through, see things through his eyes—understand that it is a hard job with a lot of pressure. If he feels your compassion, he is going to see something different in you. He'll steer you to a better deal. He'll protect you in a way he wouldn't protect other people. You'll have a more authentic experience, you'll get a better deal, and you'll have a better experience with the car after you drive away.

People in business settings default to formality rather than connection because that's been the standard for so long. Look at the way people traditionally dress for business—a suit and tie, or a skirt and blouse or pantsuit. Such formalities convey respect and professionalism, which may be a desired outcome, but such formalities can also build a wall to connection. Along the same lines, many managers are coached not to make friends with their employees, because they may have to fire them someday. There's a fear that when people get closer, respect decreases.

That's not good advice.

It's true that in the moment it may be easier to fire someone you don't know than someone you care about. You may experience more emotional hardship firing someone you really care about. But if you really love someone and are concerned about them, your decision to remove them is certain to be the correct decision because it is coming from a place of complete rectitude and understanding. If you're firing someone you don't know well, then you don't have an accurate understanding about what's going on with them. You don't know if their home life is affecting their work. You don't know if their manager is causing them to feel disempowered, and generally you lack the information you need to make a good decision.

BUSINESS IS ABOUT ABUNDANCE, NOT "WINNING"

The belief that business relationships are different from personal relationships persists in our society for a number of reasons. One of these is that many people are convinced that the way to make money is to take advantage of others. They believe that the way to get rich is to take something from somebody else. People tell themselves, "If I'm going to get really rich, I'm going to have to walk over some bodies. I am going to have to step on some people's shoulders. I am going to need a take-no-prisoners attitude." I can't tell you how many times I've heard words to this effect. What's worse, I usually hear them uttered with pride, as though "stepping over some bodies" is a sign of strength.

I'll never forget learning that Ray Kroc, credited with building McDonald's from a fledgling concept to a global brand, famously said, "If my competitor were drowning, I'd stick a hose in his mouth and turn on the water." This statement was met with praise by many who apparently thought that this "take-no-prisoners" attitude was the surest way to business success. Google it. You'll see that people have made posters of this saying, fit for hanging on a wall! This is outdated and unenlightened thinking, and just plain wrong. It is true that some have built businesses while maintaining this attitude, but their "success" was despite, not because of, their backward thinking. The exceptional success of a few people with this attitude does not prove that everyone should behave that way.

Quite the opposite is true.

Business relationships are a huge part of so many people's lives. Love belongs in business as much, if not more, than it belongs in relationships at home.

Why do I say, "if not more"?

Because we have to counter the massive, ubiquitous assumption that business means walking on people. That it means taking advantage of people. That a person can't become successful in business without making enemies. Many people assume that the way to become a leader, and the way to stay a leader, is to be powerful and to hold onto power.

Most of us have a mental picture of what people in positions of power look like. We assume, correctly, that most people in power want more power, and that the more power people get, the more they want. While that may be true for most people, that is not leadership. That's extraction. It is not supportive of what's truly important in the world. Nor is it even what is best, in the long run, for the person who's acting that way.

In fact, the best thing you can do to become and remain an effective leader is to *give power away*. The way to be the most powerful leader is to do something like what Martin Luther King or Mohandas Gandhi did. They accumulated power by giving the very power of their own vision and goals to the people around them. They gave others a vision that did not depend on them, but instead fit well with what the others needed for their own betterment. They were not financially rich, they did not display or pursue material wealth, but they became great leaders in service to others. They devoted themselves to giving away power to others, and by doing so, were able to fulfill their own goals for social change and the greater good.

The problem is that the people who are leading the top corporations and governments in the world often fail to follow in the footsteps of those leaders who tried to give away power, make others better, create win-win situations, and heal pain. When leaders actually do these things, they create abundance for everyone, including themselves.

The only source of a leader's power is that others choose to follow them. Power is not something that someone can demand. If they are demanding someone follow, or that someone obey, that is at best management, and at worst dictatorship. It is not leadership. Since the decision to follow a leader always remains with the person who follows, the best question to ask yourself is, "Why would someone choose to follow me?" The answer, in short, is that others will follow only if they trust you and believe that you will take them to a better place. Gandhi, Martin Luther King, Mother Theresa—these are people who had a vision for how things could be better and knew that their greatest reward in life would come from making the people around them better. They were people that others chose to follow. But they were not the only ones. All true leaders find powerful ways to help others.

I've been successful in business, but not by making enemies (at least that I am aware of!). I don't think anyone would say I took advantage of them in achieving success. Am I an exception? A unicorn in business? I don't think so. Like many others, I try to lead with care, concern, compassion, and love. This does not mean that I am not tough or disciplined. Quite the contrary (if you want more detail, you can read my book *Love is Free. Guac is Extra*). This approach has led me to have more success, not less—not only in business but in life. And while success must be measured by more than dollars, I honestly think that I had much more financial success with this attitude than if I'd proceeded under the old thinking that for me to win, others had to lose.

Bringing love into relationships also matters more in the business world than in other arenas precisely because it is so rare in the business world. We operate in a world of nearly unlimited abundance. By helping more people win, you win. There are more winners. There don't have to be losers for there to be winners.

Another reason love is so important in business is because work life often does not have the personal support offered by a family. You may walk into work as an employee, or as a leader, but in either case you're likely entering an environment where people don't know you as well as your partner, your family, your roommate. You are going into a place where you have less support. You may feel trepidation, anxiety, loneliness. This, then, is precisely the environment where people thirst for love, because there seems to be so little of it. If you bring love into that environment, people will respond as if you are giving them a drink in the desert.

WHAT LOVE IN THE WORKPLACE IS

The word love is fraught with many, many meanings. When I say there should be more love in the workplace, I mean we should be more caring for others, want what is best for others, be present for others, sacrifice our time and energy to help others, challenge others to be their best, develop a deep understanding of who they are and what drives them, let them know that we need them and value them.

It's a kind of love that brings discipline with it. Wanting someone to be their best, challenging them to be their best, can mean pushing them. Love isn't soft and squishy in this context. Love is about having high expectations of someone because you want them to achieve their fullest potential. Parents who love their children and expect them to get good grades are bringing discipline to their love. It's the same thing in the workplace. Loving someone means you don't settle for mediocrity when you know someone is capable of the extraordinary. Wanting what is best for someone can be felt as intense. It is direct, honest, and clear. Sometimes love means telling someone "I am committed to your success, and I will do all I can to help you, but your current behaviors are not up to the standards we expect for our team. I need you to improve for the well-being of yourself and the team. Can I count on you to do that?" If someone is still not successful in a role after a committed effort to help them succeed, love can also mean a leader must remove them from the team.

Love in the workplace means caring for others and bringing out the best in them. It means helping them become confident in their ability and encouraged by their circumstances. It means knowing them, understanding them, valuing them, respecting them, and having a deep desire to see them at their very best. Bringing all this into the workplace is bringing love into the workplace, plain and simple. You don't need to call it love. It may not even be effective or appropriate to call it love. You don't need to call it anything at all. You can just lead in a way that creates an atmosphere in which individuals tend to become confident in their ability, and encouraged by their circumstances, such that they are motivated and at liberty to fully devote themselves to the vision that you've laid out for them.

It is important to note that love and compassion do not mean lowering your standards. You could very well walk into a situation as a leader, do what I've described, and let half the team go because they are not right for the job. In fact, you might even fire people more quickly because, due to your desire to see, understand, value, and love them, you grasp that they are not in the right role for their talents, experience, aptitude, or competence. In such a situation, letting someone go is a much more loving act than coddling them and pretending that they are suited for the role if they are not. That would be dishonest, unloving, and cowardly because it would mean keeping someone in a role where they will not achieve success. Where they will not feel fulfilled, but instead will feel dissatisfied and judged by those around them. In such a situation, they won't grow to become their best. So keeping them on harms them, as well as you and your team.

VULNERABILITY IN THE WORKPLACE FOR LEADERS

Vulnerability sometimes has to be learned. I worked with a senior executive named Jeff who came across as pretty stoic and intense. His intensity could really shut others down. As part of my leadership, I had met, one on one, with every single person in every department of the company. During my time with his team I discovered that he was not connecting well with them.

I knew more about the people in his department than he did, and when he noticed this, I explained why this was the case. That I had taken the time to sit down with each of them and asked them about themselves. I'd learned what was important to them, how they felt in their position, and what their goals and dreams were. I made myself approachable, whereas he was more distant and intimidating. It's not that he wouldn't listen. He was a very intent listener. But he would stare directly at people as they spoke to them, without saying anything or making any response about what he was hearing. This had a rather intimidating effect. People speaking to him began to think he was judging them, so they tended to shut down.

Jeff was unaware of this. He wanted to appear approachable, but he didn't know how.

I told him to give his team members a "Jeff User's Manual" by explaining his idiosyncrasies. This would help them feel comfortable with him and remain open and able to connect with him. I suggested that when he sat down to speak with people, he should quickly own his behavior by telling them, "I don't think I seem very approachable. I can sort of intimidate people by how I look when I'm listening. I listen so intently that I might look angry, but I promise I'm not. This is just my resting face!"

I already was in the habit of sharing a "Monty User's Manual" with those whom I led. I often began work with a new team by first introducing myself, but then saying something like, "Hey, everyone, I talk a lot. I'm really intense. I've got a loud voice. I move my hands a lot. I'm six foot four and take up a lot of space physically. I probably also take up a lot of space psychologically. I think sometimes that's good and helpful, and sometimes it's not. I need you to help me see when it's not good and helpful. I'll try to do that myself: I'll try to beat you to it. But if you ever need to, just say, 'Monty, hold on. Can I say something?' And if you say that, it'll let me know I'm taking up too much space. Don't feel bad cutting in! You won't hurt my feelings."

It's important for everyone in a supervisory position to share their own user's manual with the people they work with. It's an opportunity to show self-awareness and to invite people to be honest and effective with you.

When you do overstep, make fun of yourself: "I'm sorry, folks. My ego got ahead of me. I got so impressed with my own story I didn't listen to you." Explain how you blew it. People love that. They'll giggle. Teach them to make fun of you. Teach them to say, "You're doing it again!"

What comes out of that kind of admission, perhaps surprisingly, is more respect for you rather than less. People know they can approach you, can contradict you, and can feel more powerful in their role. The fact that they know you want them to be powerful gives them endless respect for you. Giving a user's manual demonstrates that you are self-aware, that you lead with vulnerability, and it gives others permission to communicate with you effectively.

You may work with people who are disinclined to accept your invitation to be challenged. They may not want to take what seems like a risk with their boss. In that situation, have a direct conversation about what you want out of them: "I'm going to give you space to talk. As I try to draw you out, I'd like you to take more risks with me. Say more. Be more expressive. Risk making a mistake. Risk saying something stupid. Because I want more out of you—I'm not getting enough of what's going on inside of you, and I know you have more to offer." Then you lead by example, by being open, giving, and vulnerable.

You might read this and think, "There's no way I could do that. I'm just not wired to be vulnerable and open that way with my employees." But if you don't lead with vulnerability, be aware that your employees will have negative impressions of you. But instead of their opinions being out in the open, they'll just quietly decide you are difficult. Unapproachable. They'll talk behind your back about how you are a difficult boss. They'll make fun of you over a beer with their colleagues. What's worse for you? To try to lead a bunch of people who think you are ignorant, and make fun of you in ways you don't even know about? Or disclosing something about yourself that feels vulnerable? Trust me, the latter is better. Because guess what? They already know it anyway: they already know that you're overly intense or not a good listener or can come across as intimidating. They will figure out your weaknesses quickly, so you might as well show them that you're already aware of your shortcomings. When you do this, people will respect you, and trust that you are someone worth following.

As you advertise your own negative qualities, you demonstrate self-awareness. Self-awareness leads to respect. You get a reputation for being a self-aware person, and then your negative qualities may not even be seen as negative anymore. People will tell each other, "Yeah, he's really intense and it looks like he isn't listening well, but he's self-aware about that, and he actually is listening. You can approach him." You can turn your negatives into positives when you become vulnerable about them. You've turned the whole situation around. The people who used to talk trash behind your back now have all kinds of positive things to say to each other about you.

You may even receive letters and emails from people thanking you for showing them how to be a better person. What better way is there to show care to others than to understand and correct how your behaviors affect and influence other people?

There is nuance to being close in the right way to people you work with. If you are a leader of any kind, and you hang out with some employees but not others, there is a high likelihood that there will be an appearance of favoritism. If you are interacting socially with the men but not the women, say by playing golf together, you might be accused, even if never to your face, of sexism. There are a lot of ways things can go wrong. No matter who you are talking to, make sure you let them know the expectations for the job, that those expectations are equal for every single person who works for you, and that they will be treated fairly and equally based on their performance against those expectations, and not some other criteria.

That means you must set your expectations clearly. You must have a very clear vision. Those around you must understand that getting to know you better will not diminish your expectations of them. Make sure everyone understands why someone was promoted. Most people fail to do this, and they end up creating an aura of mystery around who is being promoted. It is urgently important that everyone has an accurate understanding of what you, as a leader, think of their performance, and that if someone is promoted, they understand why.

It's important to cultivate a culture with a high degree of openness, especially around expectations and performance. I want everyone to know my specific goals about where we're going, and I want them to have that as their own goal. If someone is not doing a good job, I want them to know. Of course, there are more and less appropriate ways to communicate that! Saying, "You're not doing a good job" is not going to inspire better performance. But sitting with someone, asking them how they think things are going, and then asking, "Can I share some things I'm concerned about?" can be effective. You can point out how the issues you're seeing are affecting the team, and how it's not helping them, either.

As you're having sincere conversations with your team, bring your innate intelligence to bear. Have conversations to understand better, but don't ask others to judge, don't share your judgment inappropriately, and don't gossip. For example, you wouldn't say to someone else, "Yeah, Bill's doing poorly, I'm going to fire him." It's appropriate to say that to someone in Human Resources. It's not appropriate to say that to someone not directly involved in his exit. That's just gossip.

VULNERABILITY IN THE WORKPLACE FOR EMPLOYEES

Using the power of love to make businesses thrive with positivity, efficiency and profitability is not only the role of leaders. Anyone can become a force for this kind of transformative change.

If you're someone in a subordinate position, and you are dealing with an intense boss or someone who is hard to talk to, you can use the same "user's manual" approach that I described for leaders in the beginning of this chapter. You can tell them, "Sometimes I have a hard time sharing with you because I'm afraid to look stupid." Or, "I don't speak up as much in group meetings because I don't want to be embarrassed, but I often get good ideas afterwards. Would it be okay if I sent you a follow-up email with my thoughts?" Or, "Yesterday you asked me a question in a meeting and I kind of froze, because I felt put on the spot. I was really nervous. I feel bad. But I've thought about your question, and I have a good answer. Can I share it now?"

As an employee, you're doing the same thing a boss could (and should) do. You're leading with vulnerability. You're giving your boss instructions on how to get the most out of you, and in so doing, you're making yourself a much more powerful, efficient, and empowered force for good. By bringing your own vulnerability into a situation, you automatically invite others to do the same, which fosters powerful and deep connections between you and those around you. Your boss likely will say something like, "Wow, I didn't think you were nervous at all, I liked what you said at the time—but tell me more!" Or, "Please don't ever think that anything you say will make you look stupid. I really want to hear your thoughts!"

By changing your behavior and bringing more vulnerability, presence and openness to your boss, your boss will come toward you. When I did this with my boss at the law firm after he slammed down a glass of water and yelled at me, my vulnerability completely changed the nature of our relationship. Permanently. It was richer, it was better personally, it was better professionally, and I advanced faster.

The same thing can happen for you.

When I worked at Dairy Queen for $2.85 an hour, I felt huge gratitude and excitement for that job. I was curious to learn and to meet people. I was enthusiastic and open-hearted. I assumed it would be fun. I expected the best of the people around me and assumed I'd like them. I was present in the moment, and I learned fast. I wanted to do each task, whatever it was, as well as I could. When I made French fries, I tried to get everything just right, from the time I cooked them, to the oil temperature, to how I seasoned them. I told myself, "It matters. It matters to people that they have a ten out of ten French fry experience." In other words, I brought a lot of positivity into the workplace.

Coming to the job with gratitude, curiosity, respect, positivity, and a desire to do your best, no matter what the job—that is what it means to bring love into the workplace. By doing this you will set yourself apart dramatically from others. You will gain the respect and gratitude of those around you. And if for some reason your approach is not met with positivity from those around you—if people are resentful or unkind—you may as well find that out quickly so you can leave and put yourself in a healthier environment. Even if you are in what people call a "McJob," if you bring the attitude I am describing, you will differentiate yourself from the people around you, and you will soon be placed into positions of greater responsibility.

Bringing love to the workplace does not mean being a pushover, or a yes-man or yes-woman. It does not mean faking agreement. It certainly doesn't mean simply doing what you're told. The idea that hiding your humanity and being more distant and formal makes you a better subordinate is wrongheaded. In fact, when you disagree, being loving requires bringing as much truth and authenticity as you can to your situation. If you are in a place of presence and love, you will sense the best and most effective way to communicate that disagreement. You probably won't say "I disagree!" Instead, you'll likely proceed with more positivity and respect, by saying, "I see what you are saying, but can I offer you another thought that I think you might like?" At any rate, you'll sense the most graceful and respectful way to bring your ideas up. If you are in a healthy culture with a healthy boss, it will go well. If you're in a terrible culture with a dreadful boss, the interaction might not feel very good—and you might decide to look for another place to work.

In a good culture, people don't treat other people like subordinates. While it is true that many managers and bosses expect a degree of obedience, that is a shame, because (as my good friend Gary Heil says) "there is no such thing as passionate obedience." Bringing humanity, bringing an open heart, and bringing presence into even the most mundane job will demonstrably raise your level of excellence.

As an employee, bring your love, fullness, presence, curiosity, gratitude, and excellence to the task at hand. Bring it to your peers, and be helpful to them. When you work better and smarter, the person next to you works better and smarter. On a Chipotle burrito line, when one employee places the rice and beans carefully on the tortilla, he sets the next person on the line up for smooth operation. When that first employee (the rice or bean person) repeats back to the customer, "Ok, you want chicken!" he not only assures the customer that they've been heard, he also sets up the next employee on the line (the chicken person) to have the chicken ready to go. Everything moves more smoothly and quickly, everyone feels good, and you end up with a nice dance down the line where each person elevates the next by doing excellent work, and the customer feels cared for.

When you make the people around you better, they notice it. They appreciate it. It's nice to feel efficient. It's nice to feel you're doing things quickly. It's nice to feel competent. That's a way of bringing love to the workplace.

I'm not naïve. I know that there are workplaces with poor cultures, where people resist change; they like things the way they are. If you come in with positivity and excellence, you may threaten them. They may think that you are making them "look bad" by comparison. They may resent that. You may get the raise they wanted. That happens—in fact, it's quite common—especially in environments that lack a leader who insists on a culture of excellence. Nevertheless, bring your best to the job. Even if the others gang up on you, keep at it. Far better to do the harder right than the easier wrong. You'll either get promoted or fired, and if you get fired, then you were in the wrong place anyway.

CHAPTER 10

Relationships with Friends

When I began taking flight lessons in Arizona, one of my instructors was a guy named Jake. At the time I was fifty years old, and he was twenty-four. I treated him like a peer more than an instructor, and we became friends. He called often to talk. He visited me in Colorado. I treated him as I treat everyone: I showed a lot of vulnerability about who I was and who I was not. I made myself very human and made myself available to him. I could tell that he appreciated this, and I noticed that he reciprocated, by making himself vulnerable as well. He shared his troubles about his girlfriend with me, the hardships of his upbringing, and even his problems with alcoholism. Jake came to really depend on me.

I share this story to illustrate what happens when you begin to make yourself open and vulnerable. You will attract new, positive relationships into your life. You will find that vulnerability makes you attractive to a wide swath of people, particularly people who have not previously experienced it and who thought that an absence of vulnerability was the normal and unavoidable state of affairs between friends. These are people who thought they had meaningful friendships but suddenly realize those relationships aren't as deep as they could be. They want more depth and see that you offer that.

In many friendships—actually in many relationships of all kinds—I see people shy away from vulnerability, even though deep inside they crave it. They may find it only in moments of drunkenness, or when they are pushed to the limits by extreme emotional or physical pain, or depression. People may briefly show vulnerability in those moments but then snap back from it, fearing the raw and sensitive feeling it gives them. For this reason, I see that most of the time people keep their relationships shallow. This is perhaps why greeting cards are so popular. People buy a card that says, "I love you" or, "You matter more to me than anyone" or, "You are the best son in the world." They let someone else say the vulnerable words for them. They sign the card, but they don't say the words themselves, because saying those words can be scary. Then they snap back to the comfort zone of not exhibiting much vulnerability in day-to-day life.

Unfortunately, this can lead people to have relationships that leave them craving something more. They want to be seen, valued, understood, and loved, but they resist allowing the requisite level of vulnerability to make this likely. In other words, they want to be fully seen, but they prevent others from really seeing them. They want to feel valued and understood, but they put up barriers that tend to interfere with others' ability to value them and understand them. They can't love a friend fully because they haven't opened their heart to let that love flow. Therefore, the other person doesn't feel the invitation to reciprocate. They end up feeling a distance between themselves and others which, while self-caused, feels lonely and cold.

It's relatively easy to make yourself open and vulnerable with a stranger you meet on an airplane and will never see again. It's much harder to contemplate doing that within an existing friendship, where you may worry that being vulnerable will somehow damage or destroy the relationship you already have, however unsatisfying it may be.

VULNERABILITY WITH FRIENDS CAN FEEL RISKY

I consider myself to be very capable of allowing vulnerability, yet while I was writing this book I realized that I had been friends with a guy for decades and never fully opened my heart to him. Somewhere along the line, I'd judged that he was a fairly private person and decided that it might make him uncomfortable if I exposed my real feelings to him. I had accommodated what I believed was his discomfort with vulnerability in order to keep the relationship safe enough for him so that he would feel good in it and not be scared away by my intensity and depth. One day, as we were having a beer, I looked him right in the eye and said, "Isn't it nice we have this friendship that's lasted so many years, where we trust each other completely, and care about, understand and value each other?"

As soon as I said this, I felt a slight pang of nervousness. It felt risky and a bit bold. For a moment, I sensed I'd crossed a line and I felt a burning sensation in my heart that matched the way I feel when I fear rejection. I looked at him and simply allowed my own discomfort to exist for a moment, to await his response.

He looked right back at me and, in a voice which sounded almost relieved, said, "Absolutely! It's awesome. I'm so grateful." His tone sounded like, "Yes! I've felt that way forever, but never knew we were allowed to say it!"

Boom. After decades, we suddenly allowed a greater degree of vulnerability, which took our relationship to another level. It felt beautiful. But the funny thing is that I realized that I had been the one, just as much as him, afraid to be fully vulnerable for fear of scaring him off. How many times do we prevent deeper connections in the name of fear? It reminds me of a time when I was in elementary school, and I had a huge crush on a girl named Holly, but I never asked her out. I once called her number, and had so much adrenaline rushing through my veins, that when she answered the phone I just hung up! Years later, she told me she had had a crush on me back then. "Oh, no!" I thought to myself. "I blew it!!"

Even for me, who touts myself to be relatively comfortable with vulnerability, exposing the real contents of my heart can be scary. In fact, even publishing this book, and thereby exposing myself to potential rejection, is scary for me! Exposing your heart might be scary for you too—scarier than it is risky, because in all likelihood it will go well. You can deepen any relationship in your life.

Go ahead and allow yourself to truly feel how much you enjoy someone. Truly feel how much you love them. You could be thinking about a friend, a co-worker, a relative. Consider whether you've placed any limitations on the relationship for fear that going deeper was too risky. Perhaps your feelings for them are deeper than what you have expressed. Then consider what it would be like to go deeper. If you really value someone, you will want what's best for that person. For your relationship to go deeper, that's a prerequisite. You will be sensitive to where they are in their journey and their life. Think about the boundaries of that relationship and whether going deeper feels appropriate. You will choose the right moment to test the waters about deepening the relationship.

Bear in mind that words are not the only way to go deeper. Sometimes you can look someone in the eye for a little longer. You can give them a hug. You can hold their hand when they are hurting or send them a card or a letter. If you are going to share vulnerability with words, it's up to you to sense the right moment. Listen to your gut, and you will almost certainly err on the side of making sure the moment is right.

The wrong moment is when you push someone into a zone of discomfort.

Commonly, this can happen when a someone misreads a friendship to have a romantic element to it when the other person does not feel that way. To deepen a relationship skillfully, you need self-awareness, and you need to be perceptive. One day I was on the golf course, and my friend and I were paired with a young man and a young woman on what looked like a first date. On the eighteenth hole, the young woman came and hugged my friend and me to say goodbye. The fellow she was on the date with chose that moment to try to get his own hug, and also to upgrade it to a kiss. It went terribly, as she pushed back, saying, "What the hell are you doing?" It was a terribly awkward moment! All because the young fellow totally failed to use his senses to feel whether the time was right. He misread the moment. He prioritized his own desire over her comfort level. Ugh! I felt bad for him, but he really brought it on himself.

People tend to operate from the perspective of fulfilling their own needs. But it's important not to allow such impulses to govern your behavior in your relationships. Honor the relationship as being important and sacred to you, and treat it that way. Come from a place not of getting, but of giving—giving your vulnerability, giving your awareness, giving your perceptions, giving your love. Do not intend, by virtue of that giving, also to take more than the other wants to give. Otherwise, you might be that guy on the golf course!

When you exhibit more vulnerability with your friends, you might notice that they begin to do it more in return, and also with their other friends. They begin to crave more depth in their friendships. They discover that being vulnerable is a catchy thing. They want more of it. They want to give more of it. If you find you have a friend you can call when you're down, a friend whose shoulder you can cry on, you find you want more of that, because it's wonderful. You'll see other relationships which lack that depth as less important. You may find, as I have, that as you cultivate deeper relationships, the people who only want to engage in small talk about the ball game or what they did last night are no longer as interesting to you. You may find these relationships less fulfilling, even a bit boring.

If any one of my relationships isn't characterized by meaningful communication, in which both of us are present and willing to share our authentic experience with each other, I will usually not be interested in devoting much time to that relationship anymore. If someone can't find their vulnerability, and keeps resorting only to small talk, I might find being around them like watching an old rerun that I am not interested in watching again. I've seen the movie *Fletch* fourteen times. It's not as funny as it was the first few times I saw it. You might find yourself in a conversation with an old friend and realize, "We're doing the same damn thing, without any advancement, every time we talk." You're watching *Fletch* again. It's stale.

A good example of this is found among drinking buddies. You may realize you have whole relationships that are based on drinking. Or smoking marijuana. Or smoking cigarettes. But you may realize at some point that such relationships are often based more on avoiding personal growth, freshness and intimacy, in favor of the preservation of a feeling of "comfort." Comfort is not a bad thing, but clinging to it too closely can present an obstacle to spiritual growth. Think about children. If you waited until they felt comfortable going to their first day of school because they were nervous, they may never attend school. Promoting their comfort in such a case would be an impediment to their development. I find that this is a major theme in society these days: people tend to work too hard to avoid uncomfortable moments for themselves and their children. But uncomfortable moments, times of struggle, are essential for our personal growth and development. We cannot coddle ourselves and simultaneously become spiritually awake! Coddling ourselves, or our children, or our minds, will necessarily limit growth. No one won a marathon without a lot of running, a lot of sweat, and a lot of discomfort.

For the foregoing reasons, it may be worthwhile to challenge how you approach your relationships. You might say, "I don't think all this drinking is so good for us. Why don't we do something different together, like go for a run?" If you end up doing that, then you can have a sober conversation where you take the relationship deeper, using all the approaches of curiosity and vulnerability I've described in this book. As with deepening any relationship, you have to take a risk, and your friend might not go there with you. They might not want to go on a run. They might not call you anymore. But that's unlikely. The likely result is that both of you will benefit.

Another place where you may see people not taking a relationship deeper is where each person, in the interest of not damaging an existing relationship, won't take the first step to go deeper—even though both of them would like to. That was the situation I found myself in with my friend of many decades. A classic example is a couple in a budding relationship. A boyfriend might want to tell his girlfriend "I love you," but he's afraid of scaring her away. She might feel exactly the same way. In the interest of not rocking the boat, neither is willing to take the risk to go deeper.

As in all relationships, humor can be an excellent tool for deepening friendships. If I say to someone I know, "Hell, we must be pretty good friends, because I'm about to show you this rash on my ass," it's both vulnerable and funny. I'm showing you my imperfect self, and I'm acknowledging the humor in that imperfection.

If we want to deepen a relationship with someone, we show them our imperfections—in effect, we show them the rash on our ass. The deeper the relationship gets, the more we are able to say to the other person, "I see you and all your imperfections, and I love you despite those. In fact, I love you more because of those."

CHAPTER 11

Relationships with Strangers

I was walking down a street with a friend in San Francisco when we passed a homeless man. He obviously was down on his luck, sitting on the steps in a doorway in the early evening. I stopped to talk to him. I looked in his eyes and saw a deep craving—not just a need for cash, or food, but also a need for connection. I asked him a little about himself, and he brightened up right away because I had taken an interest in him. After some time with him, and realizing he was hungry, I told him I was going to get him something to eat and bring it back to him.

I could see he had his doubts as to whether I'd follow through. But I did. I found a restaurant, got a takeout meal, and brought it back to him. When I returned, the surprise and delight in his expression was palpable. He probably initially thought I was just another guy giving him lip service, rather than actually caring for him. I wasn't. I could see him—really *see* him—and I wanted him to know that. This led to a long discussion, where we shared things about ourselves and developed a connection that felt valuable, genuine, and even cathartic. I felt that our interaction was rich and rewarding for both of us.

THERE ARE NO STRANGERS

I behaved this way because I don't believe in the concept of viewing other people as strangers. As you explore and find vulnerability in more and more of your relationships, you will find there is a tremendous hunger in the world among almost everyone to develop deep connections with others. We all hunger for someone to confide in, for someone to trust with our heart, for someone with whom we can share uncomfortable feelings. For someone we can take risks with and rely upon.

It's an absolute miracle that we're here. It's a miracle that we're alive. We are given the gift of that incredible miracle while being surrounded by other incredible miracles with whom we can connect and have brilliant relationships. We may let them drive us nuts. We may pick holes in them. But if we remember that each person is another miracle, we are more likely to slow down, and gain more awareness and perspective about other people, and ourselves.

Self-awareness can take the form of being able to distance oneself from one's own reputation and attachment to worldly things. For instance, sometimes when I meet people they are impressed by my material and professional success. They'll say something like, "Wow! You were the CEO of Chipotle! It's such an honor to meet you." I'll reply, "It's such an honor to meet you!" They often laugh in a way that communicates their doubt that they too are worthy of someone feeling honored to meet them, but I mean it. It really is just as much of an honor for me to meet them and connect with them as it is for them to meet me. What do my, or anyone's, worldly accomplishments have to do with how valuable it is to sit with someone and make a connection? Nothing! Once any of us bring presence to a conversation, that presence has value. It is sacred. None of us is more or less valuable because of our resume. Our value comes from our ability to be present in the moment as a loving force in the lives of others. No resume needed. Just love, authenticity, and curiosity.

The greatest hunger any of us have in this world is to feel our inherent inner brilliance: the value that each of us has by virtue of being one with the universal consciousness: one with love, and one with God. When we feel this intrinsic value, we are for that moment relieved of toil, struggle, striving, doubt, and other forms of suffering. Connecting deeply with other people is one effective way of exploring our own and another's authenticity. Connection leads to compassion, and compassion leads to love. We all fear allowing ourselves to be vulnerable to such connection, because by doing so we risk being rejected in some way by the other person. But if we cater to that fear by avoiding a connection with others, we miss one of the most beautiful opportunities to learn and grow that this life has to offer. A lot of times, in the name of emotional safety and defending our fearful egos, we don't go deeper. But when we start to go deeper with more and more people, we realize the connection that we all share. We see that in many ways we are the same. We want to feel one with the truth, love and God.

All of us have some fear that we are not worthy of being loved. That we're not really valuable. That if you really get to know me you won't care for me because you'll see that I'm not very fun, or not smart enough, not accomplished enough, not interesting enough, not cool enough. All of us have this fear. For some people, the fear is so powerful that they won't explore their own vulnerability in any relationship.

Even a single step, however small, toward vulnerability allows the possibility of a deeper connection. If we take such a step we will be rewarded, because the connections we forge will help us to deepen our connection with the very truth and love which allows us to trust and be present in our lives. All of us want the same thing, and all of us are afraid of the same things. That combination of desire and fear makes us more alike than different, whether you are the Dalai Lama or a homeless guy in San Francisco.

All of us have things we don't like about ourselves. All of us feel inferior. Sometimes we feel unworthy. All of us have these feelings in common. That means that when you meet a stranger, they're not a stranger at all. They are someone you already know quite well. You simply don't know their particulars yet.

The truth is, those particulars—in other words someone's story, or what they've done in their lives—doesn't really interest me so much. I'm much more interested in who someone is. What is their particular essence? What does it feel like to talk to them? What does it feel like to have a connection with their heart? Too often in our society, people focus on someone's story—what they do for work, where they grew up and went to school, whether they've been successful in business, and even their race or ethnicity. But their story isn't who they are. Their story is just a bunch of past experiences. Memories. History.

Most people confuse their story with who they are, but we are not our story! If you go to Disney and ride the Space Mountain rollercoaster, you are not Space Mountain. You have ridden Space Mountain, but you do not become Space Mountain. Just as riding a rollercoaster doesn't make you that rollercoaster, having a life experience doesn't make you that life experience. You are not that life experience—not that job, not that school, not that family—you are a person who has been exposed to that life experience. The person who came from that family. The person who was born that color. But your experiences cannot make a connection with another person. Only you can do that. The person who you are, not your experience, is what is available to relate to others.

A life story can be interesting, and it may give you some insight into another person. If you run into someone who has climbed Mount Everest and swum the English Channel, you might conclude they are a competitive, hard-driven person. But you wouldn't know about the underlying motivations that drive them. The interesting thing to me might be what they are running from or running toward. What's going on with them? What demons drive them? What is the vulnerability underlying their drive? Climbing Everest and swimming the English Channel are often activities that one craves to accomplish due to some feeling that is absent in one's heart. But that feeling of absence cannot be fulfilled by any worldly accomplishments. Instead, such feelings of absence can only be fulfilled by a complete surrender and acceptance of what is most true and real. What is most true and real is only available through being present and connected to the present moment, in which the substrate of the universe, love, comes flowing in.

When I meet someone, I don't see them as a stranger at all. I have just as much access to connecting with them as I do someone I've known for most of my life, because I can know them in the moment. I don't feel I know them less for not knowing their story. As soon as I look someone in the eye, I start to collect information: their willingness to hold my gaze, how they hold themselves, their posture, their smile or lack thereof. You can pick up an enormous amount of data from a person immediately if you are open and attuned. If you allow intense vulnerability, intense curiosity, and intense presence to flood those first moments of interaction with someone you've never met you will find that you can pick up most of the same clues that you can pick up with someone you've known for years.

That's why other people are not strangers. In some ways you can know them more deeply than you can know people familiar to you because you (hopefully) haven't yet saddled them with judgment or baggage. They are a fellow human being who has much in common with you, no matter their background.

We don't need to get caught up in whether what happens between you constitutes a friendship, because labels like "friendship" can get in the way of deep connection. You can have a deep connection right away. What makes someone a friend is the mutual decision to commit to keep making that connection. If you have a deep connection with someone once, and never see them again, you may hesitate to call them a friend. But you certainly had a connection.

That's why the advice I give in this book about the value of vulnerability, openness and curiosity is so relevant when you meet a stranger. If you are intensely curious, you will more likely demonstrate some vulnerability. Others will then demonstrate vulnerability in return. The connection might be very deep, very fast. Of course, as we know someone for more time, we will inevitably trigger vulnerabilities and feelings in them that might threaten that connection. In the work of getting through this, we come to know ourselves and understand our journey much more deeply. This is why longer-term relationships tend to provide the most powerful crucible for spiritual growth.

TAKE A LEAP OF FAITH

Connecting with strangers requires a leap of faith. You need to trust that everyone hungers for connection, and that it is worth the possible emotional risks to seek that connection.

That leap of faith means taking the first step and showing curiosity and vulnerability. I often deepen relationships with simple statements like, "I like being around you—let's go have a beer sometime." That's vulnerable. I've never had someone say to me, "No, I have too many friends. I don't need another one." More likely they'll say, "Sure, that sounds good." Maybe they'll call me, maybe they won't. But in my experience, leading with vulnerability is attractive and fresh to others, so usually they will be interested in pursuing a relationship.

You might experience some rejection. That's something your ego won't like, but you know what? You can handle it. You'll be fine. Rejection doesn't mean you're a bad person. It simply means that in that person's life, at that moment in time, you're not a priority. Or it means that they're afraid to go deeper—and that's not your problem. Ninety percent of the time, you'll form a deeper connection with someone, which is the most valuable thing we can have in this life.

Not every contact you have is going to develop into a deep relationship. But even casual contacts can be deeper and more rewarding when you show up, fully present, with an open heart. When you see the librarian at your town library, you can do more than just say hi and swipe your card. If you say, "Good to see you, how have you been?" and you do it genuinely, they'll see that you care. They might say, "You know, it's been tough lately." They're being vulnerable, inviting you in. You can lean in and say, "Really? Tell me about it." You don't have to spend your whole day talking to each person you meet in this way. But even short expressions demonstrating that you see and value another have the power to transform your daily interactions from robotic to spiritually enriching.

I used to go to a health club where I always said hi to Toby, a guy in his mid-sixties who manned the check-in desk. He used to say good morning and tell me a different joke each day. He learned my name. He asked how I was doing. Sometimes I might say, "I'm a little tired today," and he would push a bit. "Really? You okay?"

One day when I came into the gym, I felt particularly troubled. That day, when he asked how I was, I said, "Hanging in there, Toby." By changing my response from "Good, how are you?" to "Hanging in there," I invited him to come towards me with curiosity. I wasn't demanding his time or effort. But I was allowing for something deeper to occur. I was being vulnerable. He noticed, and he accepted my invitation.

"Really? What's going on? You seem a bit down. Are you OK?"

"Well, I'm going through a divorce. And it's a hard time."

He looked right at me and said, "Monty, it's hard, but you're going to get through it. You know why? I've been married and divorced three times, and you know what? I don't regret any of my marriages. I don't regret any of the divorces. It's okay."

That touched me very deeply. Here was a guy whose last name I didn't know. I didn't know where he lived. I didn't know what else he'd done in his life. I didn't know anything about his *story*. But that didn't matter. He had chosen to see me, and to make a connection with me.

Over the coming weeks and months, he checked in with me each time I walked into the gym. We made real connections in those moments. One moment was, for me, a particularly low point emotionally. On that occasion, he came out from behind the desk, put his arm around me and said, "I can see in your eyes that you are really hurting, Monty. I'm sorry." He had tears in his eyes. He clearly felt compassion for me. He clearly felt what I was feeling. He saw me, understood me, valued me, and cared for me. "But you are going to get through this just fine, Monty. You know why? Because you are a really good person, Monty." The way he said it felt so deep. So caring. So loving.

His words that morning moved me. This brief interaction was an affirmation which washed over me, gave me relief, and literally brought tears to my eyes. Tears of relief. Tears of being seen and acknowledged. These tears were only possible because his words had given me the space and permission to let my heart open. To trust that I could survive the pain and heartbreak I was experiencing. It showed me that the universe is filled with love and compassion. His words cost him nothing, but his concern, at that moment, was profoundly healing, enriching, and loving. It meant the world to me that he cared. Ever since, I have felt a connection and loving feeling towards him.

To this day I don't know Toby's last name. He soon left his job at the gym. I don't know where he is. But if he called me and asked me for help, I would help without thinking twice about it. I would love to be a part of his life because we shared a sacred connection. (Toby, if you're reading this, please send me an e-mail. I hope you're doing well!)

Over the course of a life built around making deep connections, I have connected with thousands of people. Sure, there's the occasional person who cuts me off in traffic—or gives me the finger when I drive poorly myself. It's true that I'm not likely to have a deep connection with them. But there are many opportunities in our lives—with the librarian, a homeless person, a grocery store clerk, a delivery person, someone sharing the sidewalk with us—where, even if briefly, we can connect.

None of them are strangers.

Conclusion

You can't have an extraordinary life without extraordinary relationships. Every part of our lives depends on our relationships with others, and learning to connect deeply with people is what leads to great relationships. Every part of our lives depends on relationships: not only our own sense of well-being, but our businesses, teams, families, and even our society. What excites me is that everyone we meet is another opportunity to establish a special and meaningful connection.

We live in a difficult time, and we need these connections, and the relationships that arise from them, more than ever.

Now...what are you going to do?

If you approach everyone you meet as an opportunity to forge a connection, not only will your life be fulfilling and rewarding, but you'll find success. You will have a more successful career. You will have deeper relationships. You will influence others. You will arrive in positions of leadership by virtue of the example you set. You will touch other people and help them reach a better place.

This is what the world needs now: for you to connect. To the people around you. To the natural world that is so in need of healing. To the infinite abundance of the universe that is truth, that is love, that is God.

Connecting to other people is a wonderful way to begin to better trust and understand the love that is the foundation of our lives. While someone's story may be interesting once, it is never the most valuable aspect of any person. What is most valuable is that they are a living outgrowth of the love that is God, manifesting in a human form, trying to rediscover their connection to God. We can be of service to them in their effort to do so. And they can be of service to us. That mutuality of service is the essence of a deep relationship, and makes our time as human beings wonderful, silly, magical, and sacred. That sacredness is what I want to be a part of. And to do so, I need to learn to be present, be aware of my ego, and learn to trust and open my heart to the authentic manifestation of others who are likewise capable.

Will you join me?

Acknowledgments

I count myself so lucky for the life I've lived, and the greatest part of my life is the love that I experience through my many relationships and friendships. I am grateful to my mother and father, who, in addition to teaching me so much about the world, also encouraged my insatiable curiosity. They somehow taught my brother and me that there was so much to life that was beyond our ready comprehension—that life was, essentially, something magical and sacred. I'm grateful to my brother, David, whose loyalty, trust and incredible humor make life feel safe and fun. I'm grateful to my many friends and my wife, who are a combination of brilliant, fun, silly, adventuresome, loyal, caring, challenging and loving, and make my life worthwhile. I am grateful to the tens of thousands of people who I have worked with over the years, some whom have led me, and others who have embraced me as their leader. I am grateful to David Chrisman, who has supported me so much in my work over the last many years. I'm grateful for my three children, Matthew, Michael, and Sara, who have challenged me, helped me to learn and grow, and brought so much love into my life. Finally, I am grateful to my editor Hal Clifford, who has patiently worked with me on bringing this book to fruition, and, while doing so, has become a valued friend.

About the Author

MONTY MORAN is a person who has a heart that is available and open. He is vulnerable and loving, and delights when those around him are at their best. He doesn't want to be known for his accomplishments, but does want to be known as someone who loves this world, and the people and animals, plants, and environment that make it so rich and special. He does not think his resume is what's important, but has still allowed us to put some of it here for the curious. Monty is the former co-CEO of Chipotle Mexican Grill. Prior to joining Chipotle, he was head of litigation and then managing partner and CEO at the Denver-based law firm Messner and Reeves, LLC, which he led for ten years. In 2020 he published his first book, *Love Is Free, Guac Is Extra: How Vulnerability, Empowerment, and Curiosity Built an Unstoppable Team*. Several years ago, Monty realized his life-long dream of becoming a pilot. Today he flies his airplane throughout the United States to pursue his interest in better understanding and serving Americans, a quest he documents through his startup, Old Tale Productions, and through his documentary on PBS, called *CONNECTED: A Search for Unity*. He is a director and chairman of corporate boards, and an advisor to many entrepreneurs and businesses. Married with three children, Monty lives in Boulder, Colorado.

CPSIA information can be obtained
at www.ICGtesting.com
Printed in the USA
BVHW040945060623
665471BV00006B/18/J

9 781544 542324